CW00487143

Usin

WordSlai 1640
on the
Amstrad PC

Using
WordStar 1512/1640
on the
Amstrad PC

Ian Sinclair

Heinemann London

Heinemann Professional Publishing Ltd
22 Bedford Square, London WC1B 3HH

LONDON   MELBOURNE   JOHANNESBURG   AUCKLAND

First published by Newtech Books Ltd 1987
First published by Heinemann Professional Publishing Ltd 1987

©Heinemann Professional Publishing Ltd 1987

British Library Cataloguing in Publication Data
Sinclair, Ian R.
Using WordStar 1512 on the Amstrad PC
– (Step by Step) 1640
1. WordStar (Computer program)
2. Amstrad PC (Computer)
I. Title   II. Series
652'.5'02855369   Z52.5.W67

ISBN 0 434 91844 X

Designed by John Clark and Associates, Ringwood, Hampshire

Printed in the UK by HGA Printing Co. Ltd, Brentford, Middlesex

Contents

Contents

Contents

Preface

WordStar 1512 is a word-processing program of formidable power from the programmers who created the whole WordStar series of word processors. Despite its familiar name, though, this is a very new product that was specifically created for the Amstrad PC1512 and, as such, it presents many features that are totally unfamiliar to any user of the older programs.

For the beginner, the suite of disks (6 in all, counting the tutorial) seems very intimidating, and the tutorial itself is a dazzling display of the features of the program. The sheer size of the program and the range of commands makes it difficult to know what is important and what is not when you first start to type modest-sized documents. In addition, the on-screen documentation does not include some features that will be important to you when you become more experienced, such as correcting words that you have added to the Spell-check dictionary, and making use of MailList dot commands.

This book accordingly sets out to describe, step by step, how to come to grips with WordStar 1512, starting with the elements of disk copying and care, and running the tutorials. From then on, you are led through the installation of WordStar 1512 for your own needs and so to the creation of simple documents, and then to the use of the more advanced features of this massive program.

The step-by-step approach ensures that you never feel lost, and can always refer back to refresh your memory on any point. It's most unlikely that anyone would ever use *all* of the advanced features of WordStar 1512, but in this book you will find all the essentials described in full detail, and the luxury features in enough detail to understand when you might need them, and how they would be used. A book like this always owes a lot to several people, and I would like to pay particular tribute to Mike Fluskey, of Newtech Books, who commissioned this book, and provided the computer and the software, and to Carol and Robin, also at Newtech, for their very considerable assistance.

Note that throughout this book, the word RETURN has been used to mean the large key on the right-hand side of the main keyboard, marked with the down-and-right arrow shape. Some texts refer to this as the ENTER key. I have also assumed that the reader knows enough about the operating system (the DOS) generally to cope with disk copying and other such 'housekeeping' actions.

IAN SINCLAIR
January 1987

PART ONE

First steps

■ SECTION 1
The tutorial

The six disks that you get as your copy of Wordstar 1512 are very precious, and you should make copies, referred to as 'backups', as soon as possible, (see Section 2).

You should certainly not make any use of these very precious disks other than to make such backups. The only exception here is that you might want to use Disk 6, the tutorial disk, to get some flavour of Wordstar 1512 before you proceed further. The other five disks do *not* provide you with word processing — they are used to create 'working' disks which you can then use.

■ SECTION 1
The tutorial

To work through the tutorial:

1 Switch the computer on, with no disk in the drive. Insert the MS-DOS system disk (Disk 1, red) when requested by the screen message

2 Remove the MS-DOS system disk, and insert your Wordstar 1512 Disk No. 6 into the drive.

3 Now type the name of the course you want. You have the choice of TUTOR, OVERVIEW, or AUTODEMO. You might want to try all three, but it's a good idea to start with AUTODEMO. Type this name, and press RETURN.

4 You will see the words 'Echo off' appear on the screen at first. Ignore this, it is simply a command that prevents the screen from showing other (unnecessary) messages. After a short time, you will see the main Wordstar 1512 demonstration appear.

5 You can make the demonstration run continously, once only, or press the ESCape key to stop the program. For a first effort, it's a good idea to make the demonstration run continuously, because you may find that you miss some points on the first run through.

6 To end the demonstration, remove all disks from the drive(s) and press CTRL ALT DEL to restart the computer. You will then need to go through all the above steps from the point where you insert the MOS-DOS system disk if you want to repeat the demonstration, or try one of the other tutorials, all of which cover the same ground.

7 A less-drastic method is to remove the demonstration disk at a time when it is not being used (Disk light out and text being written on the screen). Later, you will see the message 'Not ready error reading drive A Abort, Retry, Ignore?'. Reply by pressing the A key – you may have to do this again if the message repeats. The screen should then show A> to indicate that MS-DOS is in command, waiting for you to type another name for a program to run. NOTE: this method is more dangerous in the sense that a disk can be damaged if it is taken from the drive while the drive is still spinning. Use this method only if you are confident with the use of disks, and have a backup copy.

■ SECTION 2
Making backups

To make the backup copies, you will need to start by switching the machine on, and placing your MS-DOS System disk (Disk 1, red) in drive A when you are asked to insert a System disk.

The steps in making the copies are as follows. You might decide to copy only Disks 1 to 5, since Disk 6 is the tutorial which you might need once only. We start, as usual, with the machine switched on and the MS-DOS disk inserted when you were prompted to do so. To copy disks, you must start with the MS-DOS disk still in drive A of the computer.

1 Make sure that all of your Wordstar 1512 disks are write-protected. If they are not, then stick a write-protect tab over the notch in each disk.

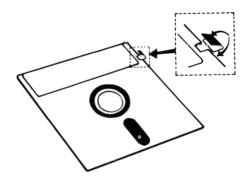

2 Type DISKCOPY A: B: and press RETURN. Don't forget the spaces — they are important. The command is the same whether you have a single floppy-disk drive or two. If you want to copy the Wordstar 1512 programs to a hard disk, use C: in place of B:. You would not normally want to copy these disks to a hard disk, however, because they are not the working copies.

3 You will then get a message on the screen about inserting disks — the actual message depends on the number of drives you have. For a twin-floppy machine you will be asked to insert the SOURCE diskette in drive A and the TARGET diskette in drive B. The SOURCE diskette is the Wordstar 1512 disk you want to copy, the TARGET diskette is a new blank disk, which does not need to be formatted.

■ SECTION 2
Making backups

4 Insert disk(s) as prompted, and press RETURN. If you have one floppy drive, you will be prompted to replace the Wordstar 1512 disk by the TARGET disk. If you are using twin floppies, you will be asked if you want to copy another disk.

5 Take out your copy and label it. Put both the copy and the original Wordstar 1512 disk in a safe place. Now insert the next WordStar 1512 disk, and (for twin drives) another blank disk

6 Answer Y to the question about copying another.

7 Repeat until all of the WordStar 1512 set of disks have been copied.

8 You now use these copies to make the WORKING DISKS or to place the working files on to a hard disk.

■ SECTION 3
Care of disks

Your disks are very precious, and most users like to have two backup sets. You should stock the original disks in a safe place which is cool, dry and well away from anything magnetic — including TV sets or monitors.

The copies are your backups which will be used to make the working disks that you will use every day that you process words. You should keep this set of backups also in a safe place ready to use if you want to make a new set of working disks or to install WordStar 1512 on to a hard disk.

You should also prepare at least six new formatted disks. To do this, you need the MS-DOS system disk in drive A, then proceed as follows:

1 Type FORMAT B: (single or twin drives). NEVER USE FORMAT C: unless you are prepared to lose all the contents of your hard disk

2 Place a new blank disk, or an old disk whose data is no longer needed, into the drive. This will be drive B if you have twin drives, or into drive A when you are asked to do so.

3 Follow the instructions on the screen, and remove the formatted disk when you are asked if you want to format another.

4 After your disks are formatted, label them as 'FORMATTED DISKS'.

You can also type an *internal* label. With the MS-DOS A> prompt showing, remove the MS-DOS system disk if it is in the drive, replace with disk you want to label, and type LABEL WSTAR or whatever name you choose. You might also like to 'label' your WordStar 1512 disk copies as WS1, WS2, and so on.

■ SECTION 3
Care of disks

Now make sure that you take good care of these, your working disks, and follow the disk care code:

■ Always make a copy of original program disks. Use the copy for your day-to-day work and store the original in a safe place.

■ Always keep at least one copy of your data on another disk.

■ Always store the disk in its paper envelope, and keep your disks in a suitable container. Store originals and copies in different locations.

■ Keep disks away from sources of heat and excessive cold. Never leave them lying on a windowsill or on top of a radiator, for example.

■ Keep disks away from smoke, dust, food and drinks.

■ Never leave disks near a source of magnetism, such as radios and telephones.

■ They may be called floppy disks but you should never bend them or put heavy weights on top of them.

■ Never touch the exposed surfaces of the disks.

■ Never switch on the computer with a disk in the drive. Always remember to remove the disks before switching off.

■ Label your disks carefully so that you know what they contain. Always write the label before sticking it on the disk. If you must write on an existing label use a felt-tip pen. •

■ SECTION 4
Installation

Before you can make use of WordStar 1512, you need to run the installation disk, Disk 1 of the set. This disk contains the codes that tailor the word-processing system to your specific requirements and create a new set of working disks that you can then use every day. The backup set that you have already made will be kept for each time you want to create a new set of working disks, or to transfer WordStar 1512 to a hard disk.

Installation is therefore a very important feature of the use of WordStar 1512, and you can't neglect it. The disks that you create during this process are specific to your computer and your printer(s), and if you change computers, you might have to make another set. Despite any message that you may read during the installation procedure, it isn't something that you can carry out in a few minutes.

Another problem arises if you are using a twin-floppy disk machine. One of the installation options when taken with a twin-floppy machine, seems to cause the installation to fail. There are no known problems with single-floppy or hard disk machines. The problem can be averted by taking a different option during installation, and this will be pointed out.

As before, you start with the computer on, and MS-DOS running, with the A> prompt mark showing on the screen. Running the installation program requires you to have *six* formatted disks ready to receive the programs. This should be in addition to the set of backup disks that you will have already made. The disks that are created from now on are your working disks. If you have no further disks to spare, then you can reformat your backup set, but this is inadvisable. You cannot make effective use of WordStar 1512 if you are going to skimp on disks!

1 With the MS-DOS disk in drive A, type FORMAT B:/S. If you have a twin-drive machine, place a new blank disk in drive B; for a single drive machine wait until you are asked to change over disks. NOTE: if you have a hard disk drive, it will be used during installation. If you do not have a hard disk, then the RAM-disk will be used. The RAM-disk size is set to 200K when WordStar 1512 is loaded in.

2 Insert the installation disk, Disk 1 of the set, in drive A.

3 Type the command INSTALL and press RETURN.

■ SECTION 4
Installation

4 You will now see a message on the screen. This asks you to press key 1 if you have a single floppy drive, key 2 if you have twin floppies, or key 3, if you have a hard disk. Press the appropriate key, but if you are not ready to go on, then press key Q to stop. Press RETURN following your choice.

5 Once you have chosen, a new message appears. You can now ask for (H)ELP, (P)ROCEED, or (Q)UIT. If you select H you can choose from another menu of general advice about such topics as filenames, RAM-disk and so on. After studying the HELP topics, you can press X to escape, and then use P to proceed with installation.

6 You are now asked to prepare your other five formatted disks with suitable labels: 1512 WP, MAILLIST, PRINTING, TEXT & DATA, and PRINTING. Write the labels, BUT DO NOT YET stick them on to the disks.If you do not have the disks ready, you can use CTRL-break to escape from the installation procedure.

7 From now on, you obey the advice on the screen, changing disks and pressing some key (spacebar is convenient) when ready. During this process, you will see the Version number of WordStar 1512. This was 1.10 for my copy.

8 Read the notes carefully before making any choice. For example, when you have to choose between Colour or Monochrome monitor, note that for the Amstrad PC1512, you ALWAYS choose Colour.

9 Where you have to choose between 'Word Processing Only' and 'WS 1512 and MailList', BE CAREFUL! Taking the 'Word Processing Only' option with a twin-disk machine seems to cause problems with the installation procedure. The problem is that when you are eventually asked to insert the WORD-PROCESSING disk, Disk 2, of the original set, the computer will not accept this disk, and repeatedly gives the 'Wrong Disk' message. There are no problems if you take the 'WS1512 & MailList' option, and no problems have been reported to date on either option when the machine is a single-floppy or hard disk machine.

■ SECTION 4
Installation

10 The first disk that is required is the '1512 SYSTEM' disk that you have formatted with MS-DOS tracks. The other blank formatted disks are needed in turn. Insert and remove disks as you are requested, and attach the label to each disk when it has been prepared. The '1512 SYSTEM' disk is needed again at the end of the installation process.

11 When the process is complete, stick a write-protect tab on to each disk. After all this, you don't want to risk them! If you want to be ultra-careful, you can make another set from this lot by using DISKCOPY — but make sure that the disks you have just created are write-protected before you do anything with them.

12 The TEXT & Data disk (Disk 5) consists of examples and demonstrations, and you will not be normally used during your work. You can make use of the files for practice purposes, and also record your own text files on this disk.

■ SECTION 5
Starting work

Now that you have prepared your set of working disks, you are ready to start work with the editing and printing actions of WordStar 1512. When you have switched on or reset your computer, you can now insert your '1512 SYSTEM' disk in place of the MS-DOS or any other System disk. This will set up the machine correctly for WordStar 1512. You can tell if the machine is ready, because the 'prompt' sign will now be A/: Using the '1512 SYSTEM' disk in this way does *not* automatically start WordStar 1512 – for a method of modifying the disk so as to do this, see Appendix A.

1 To start your WordStar 1512 program manually, type WS1512, and press RETURN.

2 You will see a screen message:

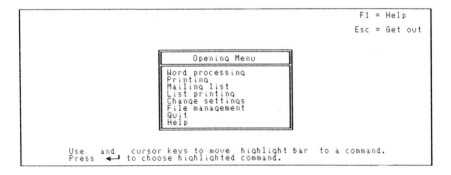

3 To start on a simple document, leave the shaded band on the words WORD PROCESSING and press RETURN.

4 The disk will spin, and will be asked to insert the disk labelled '1512 WP' into drive A.

5 Remove the '1512 SYSTEM' disk, and insert the '1512 WP' disk – the second disk that you created during the installation routine.

6 Place a formatted blank disk into the B: drive, if you have a twin-disk machine; otherwise follow the instructions on the screen. Press RETURN to start.

►

21

Starting work

7 You will be assigned a filename of PRACTICE on your chosen drive. The messages under 'File Size' will tell you how much disk space is available (362,496 characters on a fresh disk) and for what printer the page layout will be planned. The PRACTICE file is on the TEXT & DATA Disk, number 5.

8 The menu options are:

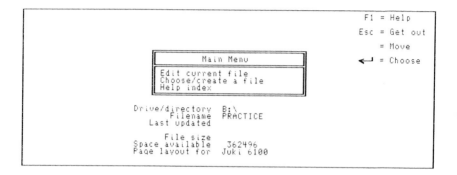

```
                                                  F1  = Help
                                                  Esc = Get out
                                                      = Move
         ┌─────────────────────────────┐         ◄┘  = Choose
         │┌───────────────────────────┐ │
         ││        Main Menu          │ │
         │├───────────────────────────┤ │
         ││ Edit current file         │ │
         ││ Choose/create a file      │ │
         ││ Help index                │ │
         │└───────────────────────────┘ │

       Drive/directory   B:\
            Filename     PRACTICE
         Last updated

             File size
        Space available   362496
        Page layout for  Juki 6100
```

9 As a first exercise, leave the shaded band over EDIT CURRENT FILE and press RETURN. You are now ready to create a document. The filename has been selected for you as PRACTICE. If you put a formatted blank disk in the drive, you will create a new file of this name, but if you put Disk 5 into the drive, you will load in a file that has already been created.

■ SECTION 6
Simple controls

WordStar 1512 emphasises the use of three keys, F1, F2, and Esc. The F1 key is used to obtain HELP, F2 to see the current menu(s) and Esc to get out of whatever you are doing.

The screen shows a simple layout. This can altered, but for the moment it can be used as it is. The bar just above the dark area is called the 'ruler' and is marked with tabulation points, spaced five characters apart.

If you press the TAB key (marked with arrows, just below the Esc key), the cursor (the flashing bar) on the first text line will move to the next TAB position, and a shaded strip will move across the ruler bar. You can return by pressing the left-arrow key (on the key at the right-hand side keypad that also carries the digit 4).

If you now type some text, you will see the text appear on the screen. You can use the key Del-left (marked with Del and the left-facing arrow) to erase any mistake. DO NOT press the RETURN key until you reach the end of a paragraph. You do not need to press any key to move one line to another, since this is done for you.

After you have typed some text, like this:

```
                                          F1 = Help
                                          F2 = Other menu
                                         Esc = Get out

                  Page 1 Line 3 Col 08  Insert ON
_____ _____ _____ _____ _____ _____    Editing Menu - 1 of 2
   This is some practice text created in a first attem
aaaaaa n be moved with the keys that are marked xxxxx x   Boldface
You canaaaaaa aaaaaa  check the spelling of this text b   Underline
F2 twice and selecting 'Spelling Correction', but remem   Move text
this takes time, and needs a change of disks.             Copy text
                                                          Delete text
                                                          Restore deleted text
                                                          Temporary indent
                                                          Paragraph re-form
                                                          End page
                                                          Save
```

press Esc. You will be asked if you want to 'Save changes' or 'Abandon changes' The shaded band is over 'Save changes', and this is the normal position.

Press RETURN to save the file PRACTICE on to the disk that you are using for text. If you use a twin-drive machine, this will be the disk in drive B. If you are using a hard disk machine, this will be the disk in drive A. If you have a single floppy drive, you will be prompted to change disks.

➤

■ SECTION 7
Moving through a file

Before you can obtain any practice in using the cursor commands you need a file to work with, and it's much too laborious to have to type a lot of text on Disk 5. An alternative, which is more interesting, is to look at the commands that are part of your installation disk. This particular text may not make very much sense when you first see it, but there is enough of it to make a large example.

Load the text called INSTALL2.BAT as follows:

1 Start WordStar 1512 in the usual way. When you see the table of word-processing options in the Opening menu, choose word-processing.

2 Insert your copy of the installation disk, which should be write-protected, into the drive that you use for the text.

3 Take the option of 'Choose a file to edit/create'. You will see a list of files.

4 Use the down-arrow key or move the mouse to shift the shaded bar to INSTALL2.BAT.

5 Press RETURN. You will then see the text appear on your screen.

24

■ SECTION 7
Moving through a file

With this text in place, you can now see how to move the cursor to any part of the text. This is important because editing is carried out at the point where the cursor is placed. The cursor-moving commands of WordStar 1512 allow you to place the cursor anywhere you like in the text. You should try each of these actions as described below until you are familar with them.

■ The simplest cursor moving keys are the arrowed keys, on the numbered keypad at the right-hand side. As an alternative to these keys, you can use the mouse.

■ The right and left arrow keys move the cursor by one character, in the direction of the arrow. You cannot move further left than the left-hand margin, but you can move beyond the right-hand margin.

■ When you move beyond the right-hand margin, the shaded strip on the ruler bar remains at the right-hand side to remind you.

■ The up and down arrow keys move the cursor in the direction of the arrow by one line at a time.

■ All of the arrowed keys, like the other keys, repeat if you keep them depressed, so that you can move through a file just by keeping a key depressed.

■ There are, however, much better ways of moving the cursor over larger distances.

■ SECTION 8
More movement

■ You may need to move from the top to the bottom of a document. This is done by pressing the **Ctrl-PgDn** keys. This means that you press the Ctrl and PgDn keys at the same time. Don't be surprised when you hear the disk spin, because WordStar 1512 keeps text stored on the disk until it needs it.

■ To move back to the top of a document, press **Ctrl-PgUp**. This time, you will not hear the disk spin if the document is short, because the whole of the text has been loaded into the memory.

■ It's very useful to be able to move word-by-word. You can do this by using the **Ctrl** key along with an arrow key, right or left (up/down arrow keys have no effect when used Ctrl).

■ You can move to either end of a line by using **Ctrl** with **Home** or **End**. Pressing Ctrl-Home takes the cursor to the left-hand side of a line. Pressing Ctrl-End takes the cursor to the right-hand side of a line.

■ The **Home** key, used alone, takes the cursor to the start of the top line on the screen. The **End** key, used alone, takes the cursor to the start of the line above the bottom line.

■ The **PgUp** key, used alone leaves the cursor in place, and moves the text by 19 lines *down* past the cursor. The **PgDn** key, used alone, also moves the text past the cursor, but in the opposite direction, so that the text moves *up* past the cursor.

That's it! You now know the cursor-moving commands. These are the commands you will use most of all as you edit text, so that the more experience you get with them the better. The mouse can be used, but it is much more difficult to control the position of the cursor with the mouse. With the sample text that you now have in the memory, you can practice as much as you like.

When you have finished, you should abandon the file. This is in case you have altered it in any way, because if you replaced this file in an altered form, you might not be able to install further disks. Your write-protection on the disk should prevent this in any case, but to get used to the form of the abandon command, try it now.

Press the Esc. key, and move the shaded bar over the words 'Abandon changes', Press the RETURN key.

NOTE that dates that are displayed by WordStar 1512 are in US form — giving month number/day number/year, and the times are in AM/PM form rather than 24-hour clock.

■ SECTION 9
Deleting text

You need to be able to delete text as part of editing, and now that you have experienced the ways in which the cursor can be moved, we can look at how the text at the cursor position can be deleted.

■ The simplest deleting actions are the character deleting actions. At the top right-hand side of the main keyboard, there are two **Del** keys, one marked with a right-facing arrow, the other with a left-facing arrow. We will call these **Del-right** and **Del-left**, repectively. There is also another Del key on the bottom row of the numberpad, next to the key marked Enter. We'll refer to this key as simply the **Del** key.

■ The **Del-right** key *has no effect* when you are using WordStar 1512. The **Del-left** key will delete the character immediately to the left of the cursor. The **Del** key (on the number keypad) will delete the character that the cursor is over.

■ All of these key actions will repeat if you hold a key down, so that you can delete several characters backwards by holding down the Del-right key, and several characters forwards by holding down the Del key. Try this with some text, using the PRACTICE file or the INSTALL2.BAT file.

■ WordStar 1512 has provisions for deleting more than one character at a time, however, and you should try the following:

1 Place the cursor along one of your text lines, away from the left-hand side. Now press Ctrl-Del-left (the Ctrl key along with the Del-left key). This will delete all of that line that lies to the left of the cursor. The remaining lines will move to fill up the gap – an action called auto-reformatting.

2 For deleting larger amounts of text, press F2 to get the Editing Menu, and move the shaded bar, using the arrowed keys, to the DELETE TEXT option. Press RETURN. You are asked to move the cursor to the start of the text that you want to delete and press RETURN again. The text is marked as you move the cursor from the start to the end of the section.

3 The 'deleted' text is temporarily held in the memory, and can be restored either where it came from or at another place. To do this, press F2 again, and select the RESTORE DELETED TEXT option. You will be asked to move the cursor to the place where you want to put this text, then press RETURN. Note that only the most recently deleted text can be restored. You cannot restore text that was deleted earlier unless it has been saved on disk (details later).

27

PART TWO

Taking more control

■ SECTION 10
Printing the file

When you have created a file of text, that text resides normally on the disk and you can load it in again for further editing as you please. Unlike using a typewriter, you do not print text from a word processor until you are ready to do so. This will be when you are completely satisfied that the text is exactly as you want it. Unless the text has been saved on to a disk, you cannot print it. To print a text file, proceed as follows:

1 Make sure that your printer is connected and switched on. The printer must be of a type that was specified during installation.

2 Get to the opening menu of WordStar 1512. If you have just loaded the first disk, the opening menu will be on screen. If you haved just completed editing the file, press Esc so as to bring up the opening menu.

3 Move the cursor over the option PRINTING, then press RETURN.

4 You will be asked to insert the PRINTING disk, Disk No. 4, into drive A. Do this, and then press RETURN.

5 The Print menu will appear.

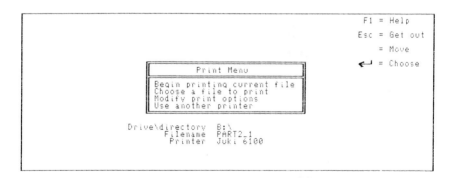

6 If you have just finished editing a file, this will be the 'current file' and selecting this option, by pressing RETURN, will print the file. If the printer is switched off, the file will not be printed, but WordStar 1512 will show the printing as proceeding.

7 If you want to print a different file, you can take the second option in the Print menu, CHOOSE A FILE TO PRINT. Taking this option will present you with a directory listing, and allow you to type the name of a file. When you press RETURN, this will be made the current file.

8 The third choice is of Print options.

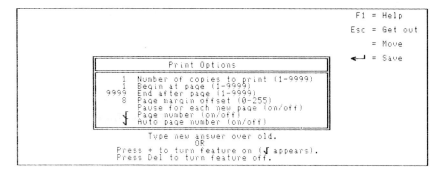

```
                                          F1  = Help
                                         Esc  = Get out
                                              = Move
                                         ←┘   = Save

   ┌────────────────────────────────────────────┐
   │          Print Options                      │
   ├────────────────────────────────────────────┤
   │     1   Number of copies to print (1-9999)  │
   │     1   Begin at page (1-9999)              │
   │  9999   End after page (1-9999)             │
   │     8   Page margin offset (0-255)          │
   │         Pause for each new page (on/off)    │
   │    √    Page number (on/off)                │
   │    √    Auto page number (on/off)           │
   └────────────────────────────────────────────┘
           Type new answer over old.
                       OR
        Press + to turn feature on (√ appears).
        Press Del to turn feature off.
```

You will not normally need any of these for short documents, but for longer documents, you might need the Pause for each page option. If you are using single sheets, as opposed to continuous stationery, on your printer, you will want the printer to pause at the end of each page so that you can change sheets. To do this, move the cursor down to this line, and press the + key (either + key can be used).

9 You can also opt to use another printer. The choice is of the DMP3000 (Amstrad) or a third type, and if you want to use an Epson dot-matrix printer, then the DMP3000 setting will provide for this to some extent. This option allows you the choice of another printer for a fast trial copy before committing you to a final printout with the slower daisywheel. (See Section 24 for details of how to include the Epson or any other printer into this list.)

10 When you finally select the file to print, press RETURN to start printing, and you will see your file printed. The example shows a short file printed with the Juki 6100 daisywheel printer.

This is an example of text that has been created, edited, and then saved to a disk. Following saving, the text has been printed, as shown here. The installation procedure specified a Juki 6100 daisywheel printer, and this is the printer that has been used. The daisywheel is a 10-pitch type (character spacing normally 10 per inch), but the settings of the printer permit operating with the same type size closer spaced at 12-pitch (12 characters to per inch). This has been selected because it gives neater printing. The default settings of WordStar 1512 have been used.

■ SECTION 11
Page size

The use of A4 paper with normal print sizes is enough for many purposes, but WordStar 1512 would hardly be considered much of a word processor if it did not allow you to make provision for other paper sizes and layouts. The most common sizes are shown here in the illustration.

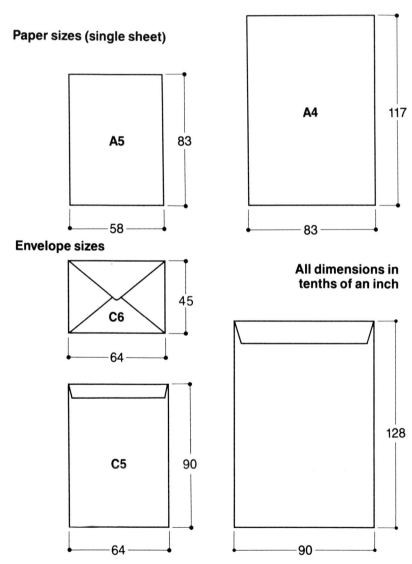

Paper sizes (single sheet)

A5   83   58

A4   117   83

Envelope sizes

C6   45   64

All dimensions in tenths of an inch

C5   90   64

128   90

Papers – continuous

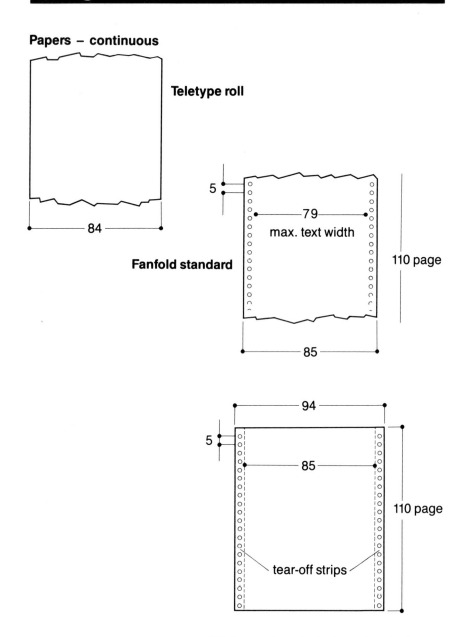

Teletype roll

84

Fanfold standard

5

79
max. text width

110 page

85

94

5

85

110 page

tear-off strips

All dimensions in tenths of an inch

■ SECTION 11
Page size

Unfortunately, changing settings with WordStar 1512 is not always a simple matter. The following example shows how to change margins to give 42 characters per line on A5 paper. The reason for the choice of 42 is that A5 paper is 5.8 inches wide, allowing a maximum of 58 spaces. The printer settings normally allow a margin of 8 spaces at the left hand side, and to make the text look balanced, you should allow the same margin at the right, so leaving 42 characters in the line.

Changing settings is easier if there is no text being worked on. The following procedure assumes that you have cleared out any text. Make sure the text is recorded, and then pick the Delete option from the menu that you get by pressing F2.

1 With the text deleted, press the F2 key until you get the second page of the Editing menu.

2 Pick the TABS AND MARGINS option, and press RETURN.

3 Move the cursor right until the Col number is 42, then type R. This will set the right margin to 42, with the left margin unchanged.

4 You very seldom need to change the left margin setting, but if you want to do so, you position the cursor and then type L. If you want printed output to have a different margin, it's always better to alter the printer margin setting.

5 When you press RETURN, the new margin setting will appear. You can now type new text, or insert text from another file. New text will appear between the correct margins.

This is an example of text that has been created, edited, and then saved to a disk. Following saving, the text has been printed, as shown here. The installation procedure specified a Juki 6100 daisywheel printer, and this is the printer that has been used. The daisywheel is a 10-pitch type (character spacing normally 10 per inch), but the settings of the printer permit operating with the same type size closer spaced at 12-pitch (12 characters per inch). This has been selected because it gives neater printing. The default settings of WordStar 1512 have been used.

■ SECTION 11
Page size

6 If you want to insert text from another file, press F2 to get the Editing menu, and select the INSERT A FILE option. When you press RETURN, you will be asked to place the cursor where you want the file inserted. Move the cursor to the start of the page, and press RETURN again. This brings up the directory so that you can choose which file to insert.

7 An inserted file will not show the correct margins until you reform it. Press F2 twice, and select PARAGRAPH REFORM, then press RETURN. You have to select 'paragraph reform' for each paragraph that you want to change to the new margins. Don't be alarmed by the appearance of the text after reforming – press PgUp to restore normal appearance.

IMPORTANT NOTE:
Unless you are working with very short documents, the file to be inserted **must** be on the same disk as the file you are creating. If you want to insert from several disks, use file management (see Section 33) to copy files to drive C (single or twin disk machine) or drive D (hard disk machine) before starting editing.

■ SECTION 12
Tabulation stops

As well as changing margins, you can change the tabulation stops (represented as downward-facing arrows) in the ruler line. This can be done at any time, whether text is present or not. From the opening menu, choose a new file name, so that the program starts with no text. As an example, set up tabulation for a short memo on A5 paper, using a right margin at column 42 as in Section 11. Now proceed as follows:

1 Press F2 until you reach the page which includes the TABS & MARGINS option, and select it by moving the shaded band and pressing RETURN.

2 After setting the right margin to column 42 (see Section 11), delete the tab stops between the margins. Do this by placing the cursor over a tab stop and pressing the C key. You need to do this for each tab stop separately, since there is no command for deleting all tabs.

3 Now set new stops. Place the cursor at column 2, and press the T key to set a tab stop. Similarly, set tab stops at column numbers 4, 6 and 21.

4 Now each time you press the TAB key (under the Esc key), the cursor will move to the next tab stop on the right. This allows you to line up text neatly, as the following MEMO example shows:

```
                     MEMO
     This  has  started  on  the  TAB  stop  at
column  2,  with  the  right  margin  set  to  42
for  A5  paper.
     By  using  two  presses  of  the  TAB  key,
this  paragraph  can  be  started  at  column  4,
which  might  be  useful  for  emphasis.
     We  can  also  use  the  tabulations  for
lining  up  other  items:
          Items  like  this
          in  columns
          like  lists.
     And  the  centre  tabulation  can  be  useful
for  ending  a  memo  -
                    P.  Fotheringay,
                    Head  of  Section.
```

■ SECTION 13
Decimal tabs

Decimal tabs allow you to line up numbers so that the decimal points are in a vertical straight line. This is particularly useful for money amounts. In the ruler line, the decimal tab appears as a 'hash' sign, #. This sign is sometimes referred to in US manuals as the 'pound' sign, and in many programs, including WordStar 1512, you may find that the English pound sign will print as a hash sign.

To try the effect of decimal tabbing, set up as usual with no text and use the F2 key to choose the TABS & MARGINS option.

1 Delete other tabs, set margins and select normal tabs in the usual way.

2 Place the cursor where you want the decimal tab. In the following example, the decimal tab has been placed at column 26. With the cursor in place, press D to put in the decimal tab, #. Note that you do NOT press the # key.

3 Return to normal text entry and type some text and numbers, as the following example. When you tab over to the decimal point, each character you type will appear at the position of the decimal point. Previous characters in that line will be shifted left until you type the point. After the point has been typed, characters appear to the right of the point. You must NOT include a space in anything that you want lined up in this way.

4 Words can also be lined up, because the full stop is the same character as the decimal point. You cannot, however, line up phrases because the use of a space destroys the effect of the decimal point.

■ SECTION 13
Decimal tabs

This example uses the decimal tab set at column 26 so as to allow neat arrangement of numbers, particularly money amounts.
        For example:
                        #35.67
                        #423.03
                        #12.90
- and we can also use any other quantities that involve decimal points, such as -
                        0.0017"
                        16.413 m
                        22.504 kg
- or whatever we like. To use the decimal stop, we need to tab to the position of the decimal tab, and then enter the amount. The digits will be lined up whenever the decimal point is used. You can use only one decimal tab, and line up only one decimal point in each line.

The decimal tab will also line up words so that a full-stop will be placed under the decimal tab.
                        First.
                        Second.
                        Third.
                        Fourth.
- but you cannot line up anything that includes a space, because using a space stops the action of the decimal point.

■ SECTION 14
Centring text

Very often it is useful to be able to centre text in its line. This can be done manually because it's so easy to adjust the position of text, but a better method is automatic centring. This makes use of another option in the menu that is obtained by pressing the F2 key.

1 Type the phrase that you want to have centred. The phrase must fit within a line.

2 Leave the cursor at any point in that same line.

3 Press F2, and select the CENTRE LINE option. This will often be the default, because it's the first item in the list.

4 Press RETURN to confirm the selection. You will see a screen message asking you to place the cursor anywhere on the line you want centred, and press RETURN. Press RETURN again at this point.

5 The text will be centred. If the cursor has not moved to the next line, you will need to press RETURN again.

```
                      MEMORANDUM
    This shows the use of centring on a line
of text. You can also centre phrases:
                        Name
                Address First line
               Address second line
                     and so on.
    The procedure is rather clumsy, because
you need to press the f2 key, then RETURN
(twice) to centre each phrase.
Fortunately, the Centre Line option is the
first in the list, so that you don't need
to spend much time searching for it.
```

■ SECTION 15
Temporary indent

Another useful addition to your repertoire of effects is paragraph indenting. Line indenting means that a line starts to the right of the normal left margin, and this is achieved simply by using the TAB key. Paragraph indenting means that each line in a paragraph will start at a new left margin to the right of the normal margin. You can use paragraph indenting on new text, or on text that has already been typed without switching on paragraph indenting. The use of paragraph indenting is a very good way of emphasising a paragraph, or indicating that the paragraph is a quotation or otherwise not a normal part of the text.

1 For new text, press F2 to get the first Editing menu, and select TEMPORARY INDENT. Press RETURN.

2 You will be asked to move the cursor to the beginning of the text you want to indent, and press RETURN. The indenting will be to the first TAB stop. Indenting ceases when you press RETURN.

3 To indent an existing paragraph, select the TEMPORARY INDENT option, and place the cursor at the start of the paragraph, then press RETURN.

4 You will not necessarily see the paragraph indented completely until you use PARAGRAPH REFORM, which is the next option down in the Editing menu.

5 If you type anything else into an indented paragraph after completing it, you may find that the indenting disappears. Use TEMPORARY INDENT and PARAGRAPH REFORM again if this happens.

■ SECTION 15
Temporary indent

The normal start to a paragraph is an
indent, which can be obtained by using the
tabulation key at the start of the paragraph.
Some word processors allow for this
automatically, and make the cursor move to
the appropriate position on a new line
whenever the RETURN key has been pressed.
  By using the temporary indent of WordStar
  1512, you can make each line of a paragraph
  become indented as compared to the rest of
  the text. This indentation is temporary in
  the sense that it will cease when you use
  the RETURN key to start a new paragraph.
Thus, this line has started at the normal
left hand side, because the temporary indent
is finished, and the TAB key has not been
used. Notice the symbol on the right-hand
side of your screen which marks the end of
each paragraph (each time you have used the
RETURN key).

■ SECTION 16
Text enhancement

There are very few types of printers that do not allow some forms of text enhancement. By enhancement, I mean the use of **bold type,** underlining and so on. The choice of enhancements is limited to what your printer can achieve, so that anything other than boldface and underline may not be possible if you are using a daisywheel printer. If you are using a dot-matrix type, such as an EPSON, a huge variety of enhancements may be possible. These are not so easy to achieve with WordStar 1512, and are not dealt with in this Part.

The use of boldface and underlining is dealt with from the normal editing menu, in the first group of options. You can emphasise a word you are about to type, or one that you have just typed.

1 To use boldface, press F2 to get the menu, and choose the BOLDFACE option. You will be asked to move the cursor to the start of the emphasised section, and then press RETURN. If you are about to type the word, press RETURN and then type on. The words that you type will appear in inverse video, meaning dark lettering on a light background.

2 The effect continues until RETURN is pressed again. You move the cursor, or type on, until you want to stop the enhancement, and then press RETURN again. The word(s) that you have enhanced remain emphasised in brighter print in the text.

3 To underline, follow the same procedure, but use the UNDERLINE choice from the F2 menu. When you stop underlining, the words appear only very slightly brighter than the surrounding text, and this is easily missed.

Text sometimes needs **emphasis,** and the use of bold face print is a particularly useful way to achieve this. Another method is underlining, and either effect is marked in the text by the use of brighter text.

Text enhancement

Note that these and other enhancements of text can be combined:

Normal text
Boldface
Underline

Subscript
Superscript

Boldface and underline

Boldface and subscript
Boldface and superscript

Underline and subscript
Underline and superscript

Boldface, underline and subscript
Boldface, underline and superscript

You need to be careful about deleting bold or underlined text. An invisible code number is placed at each end of such text and you must make sure that these codes are deleted. If you want to delete the whole section that is emphasised, then just make sure that you have deleted from the start of the following word to the end of the previous one. For example, if you had the line:

This is **emphasised** text

— you should delete so that it looks like:

This istext

— and then put in the space. If you leave any spaces, they may contain invisible codes.

You can check for codes by watching the left-hand side of the strip at the top of the screen. When the cursor is over a code, the word corresponding to the code will appear (Boldface, Underline, etc.). You can then use the Del key to remove the code. You *must* remove both codes if you want to remove emphasis but retain the text that was emphasised.

■ SECTION 17
Superscript and subscript

Text sometimes needs the use of subscripts and superscripts. A subscript is a letter, number or word that is printed slightly lower than the normal line position, and a superscript is printed slightly higher. The effects do not appear on the screen, and will appear on paper only if your printer supports this effect.

Printers achieve the effect by rolling the paper slightly on (for subscript) or back (for superscript) and returning to normal setting at the end of the emphasised section. Most printers are capable of this type of action, though many daisywheel printers use a movement of half the normal line spacing, which is rather more than is needed. This can cause text to look ugly if a subscript on one line meets a superscript on the line below. Such text should be printed with double line spacing, or with the superscript and subscripts in smaller font (see Section 25).

To achieve sub- or superscript:

1 Use F2 and choose the required option, then press RETURN.

2 Press RETURN at the start of the sub-/super- section. This can be existing text, or text that you are about to type.

3 At the end of the section, press RETURN again. The affected text appears in slightly darker colour – very difficult to distinguish.

4 To check for the existence of sub-/super- text, move the cursor to the first or last character and look for the message at the left hand side of the top of the screen.

5 To delete the sub-/super- text, or to retain the text and cancel the emphasis, see the remarks in Section 16. There is an invisible coded number at each end of the text, and both codes need to be deleted.

➤

■ SECTION 17
Superscript and subscript

Some printers allow text to be ~subscripted~
or ^superscripted^. This is done by moving
the print roller up or down by less than
the normal line spacing. You need two
steps to delete these instructions, once
at the start and once at the end of each
section.

Subscripts and superscripts are used
mainly in text that deals with mathematics
and chemistry, and for normal purposes,
you may never need to use these effects.

■ SECTION 18
Line spacing

For many requirements, text has to be double-spaced, meaning that a blank line has to be left between each pair of text lines. This is particularly important for manuscript that is to be submitted for publication either in a magazine or as a book. Publishers like you to use wide margins, A4 paper, printed one side only, and double-line spacing, since this leaves room for sub-editors to 'mark-up' the text. The only time when you can use single-spacing for text that is to be published is when you are using 'desktop publishing', delivering the text on disk to be printed as you have typed it.

1 Select the Line spacing option from the Editing menu after pressing F2. You will be asked to select single-, double- or triple-spacing. Use triple only for text that will need a lot of marking-up, like mathematical or chemical material.

2 When you have selected the spacing that you want, press RETURN.

3 Text that you type from this point will use the new spacing. You can return to single spacing by using the F2 menu again.

4 If you have existing text that is in a different spacing, you can change spacing, and then use PARAGRAPH REFORM to alter the spacing of the existing text, paragraph by paragraph.

5 Note that WordStar 1512, unlike most word-processing programs, shows the double/triple-spacing on the screen.

■ SECTION 18
Line spacing

This text is typed using double spacing, typical of text that is intended for publication. WordStar 1512 shows the double spacing on the screen, unlike most word-processors which carry out the double spacing only when the text is printed. If your existing text is single-spaced, you can select double (or triple) spacing and alter the existing text, one paragraph at a time, by using the **paragraph reform**.

The use of double spacing often makes text easier to read when you are entering it, but you see very little of your text on each screen 'page'.

■ SECTION 19
Making pages

Longer texts need to be split into pages. The standard settings of WordStar 1512 allow for 66 lines per page, with the left, right, top and bottom margins suitable for A4 paper. We shall look at how to alter these settings later in Section 22. In the following example, the lines-per-page setting has been altered to 7 lines so as to illustrate the effect of paging.

■ As you type text, you press the RETURN key only when you want to start a new paragaph. Words are never split at the end of a line, they automatically move to be next line if there is no room for them. This is called 'word-wrap'.

■ When your text is at the end of a page, you will see a pair of lines stretching across the width of the screen, marking the page boundary.

■ Having a visible page boundary like this allows you to adjust text so that it is not awkwardly split across pages.

■ You can force a new page to be taken by using the PAGE END option after pressing F2. When you use this, you will see **.pa** appear in the text, and the page boundary under it. The .pa is not printed, it appears only as a message on the screen.

■ You can also force a new page to be taken by typing .pa as the first and only item on a line. This works only if the dot is typed on the first possible space, column 01.

■ If you type a dot in column 01 by mistake, any text following it will not print normally, since this dot position is taken as the start of some form of instruction. For further details of such 'dot commands' see later, Section 40.

➤

■ SECTION 19
Making pages

This has been typed with reduced width and

double spacing, with the selection of only 7

lines per page. In this way, we can

illustrate the action of paging, and using

1

the End-page option.

2

This is a line - now type .pa on the start of

the next line

3

4

PART THREE

Using the printer

■ SECTION 20
Paper and printer

It's time now to look at the settings for the standard page of WordStar 1512. As you have typed words on to the screen, and recorded them on disk, these words are organised into lines and into pages automatically by the program when the text is printed.

You can change the number of characters that you put on to a line by means of the F2 menu as you prepare to type the text, but such changes do not alter the number of lines on a page, nor the way that the printed page is laid out other than its number of characters per line.

■   The **normal page standards** of WordStar 1512 are shown below:

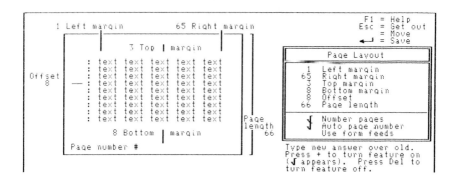

■   The **settings** are recorded on the 1512 System disk, so that they are automatically used by the system whenever you load it. As we shall see, if you need to use more than one type of page layout, the ideal method is to prepare one 1512 System disk for each layout.

■   The figure for **offset** means the number of character spaces between the left-hand side of the paper and the theoretical start of text. These spaces are each a tenth of an inch wide, so that an offset of 8 means 8/10ths of an inch in from the left-hand side. This is the quantity that we would normally refer to as the left margin.

■   Added to this offset is the **left margin**, normally set at 1 — you cannot specify anything less. The position of the first character on paper, then, is the sum of offset and left margin, a total of 9/10ths of an inch in the standard settings.

Paper and printer

■ The **right margin** figure represents the position of the right-hand side of the text *measured from the left margin*. This implies that the position from the left-hand edge of the paper is 9 + 65 = 74 characters, or 7.4 inches.

■ The **top** and **bottom margins** are measured in terms of standard lines, assuming 6 lines per inch. Each unit therefore is of 1/6th of an inch.

■ A **top margin** of 3 therefore represents half an inch (3/6ths), but this by itself is misleading. When you put paper into a printer, it will normally be placed so that the top edge of the paper is 1 inch above the printer head, and this distance must be added to the top margin unless you can place your paper differently. The total top margin is therefore 1.5 inches.

■ A **bottom margin** of 8 spaces represents 1.34 inches.

■ A **page length** of 66 means 66 lines of total text space, including the top and bottom margin figures. Since these margins amount to 11 lines, then a page of 66 lines will contain only 66-11 = 55 lines of real text.

■ You can alter any of these number settings, as we shall see in the following section, but only numbers that are acceptable can be entered.

■ The standard settings also include automatic page numbering, with the page number placed on the bottom line and centred.

■ SECTION 21
Page layout

You can work with the standard settings and still cope with odd pieces of work on other paper sizes, such as A5, by altering margins and being careful about lines per page. For anything other then the occasional single page of non-standard size, however, you need to change the Page layout settings. This is done by using the CHANGE SETTINGS menu:

1 Save any text that you have been working on, and get to the opening menu. If you are using the editing menu, then press the Esc key until you see the opening menu.

2 Place the shaded bar over the CHANGE SETTINGS option, and remove the 1512 WP disk from drive A. Put in the 1512 System disk. Press RETURN.

3 You will see the Change settings menu:

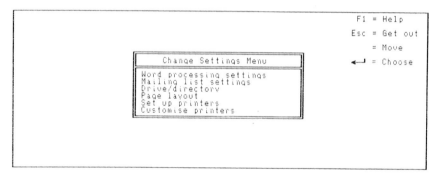

4 Move the shaded bar to PAGE LAYOUT and press RETURN.

5 You will see the page layout (as in Section 20) illustrated on screen. Note these standard settings, because if you change them you may want to use the originals again.

6 The CHANGE SETTINGS menu also allows a number of other changes to be made. All of these changes are recorded on to the 1512 System disk so that they become your new standards each time you start using WordStar 1512.

7 If you need to work with several different settings, then it's usually easier to make a different 1512 System disk for each one rather than altering the settings each time you need to change.

■ SECTION 22
A5 settings example

In this section, we'll illustrate the use of changing settings to accomodate A5 paper. Before starting, switch to the CHANGE SETTINGS menu as noted in Section 21, and make a note of the standard A4 settings of the Page layout menu.

1 Draw out the new standards that you will need. A5 paper is 58 characters wide, so that narrower margins should be used.

2 Before you start to change the layout, you will be asked to choose a printer. The first-choice printer is automatically shown as the Amstrad DMP 3000, and the second choice will be the printer that you specified during installation. Place the shaded bar over this printer name before proceeding. Choice of printers will be dealt with later, Section 24.

A5 settings example

3 When you reach the Page Layout menu, you can start to fill in the figures shown in the drawing above. As usual, you can move the shaded bar to the figure you want to change, type in the new figure, and move the shaded bar to another figure. You should end up with the scheme illustrated here:

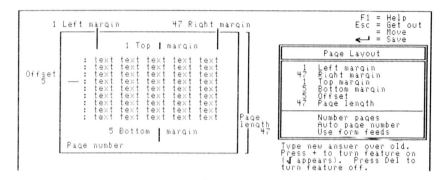

4 When all the figures for the new layout have been entered, press RETURN to record the data on to the 1512 System disk. Each time you edit a document from now on, the new layout will be used. Old text read from the disk will also be forced into the pattern of the new layout.

5 If you want to return to the original A4 layout, you will have to repeat the steps in this section, typing in the figures for the A4 layout.

Here is some text printed using the A5 layout. Note that the page number is placed at the bottom of the page, and you will need to ensure that the paper is put carefully into the printer in order to see the page number at all. If the top of the paper is even fractionally high, then the page number will be off the bottom edge.

This has been typed in A5 format, with
double line spacing used. The Page layout menu
has been used to make the changes that are
needed for working with this size of paper, but
no changes have been made to the Printer setup,
so that pages will be printed to the correct
size, but the feeding will be incorrect.

The aim of using the Page layout for A5 is
to ensure that the correct page breaks are
shown, and that the margins are set
automatically without any need to use the
Margin & Tab menu. You can still use the Margin
and Tab. menu to change to other settings for a
document or part of a document, but each time
you create a new document, or edit this one,
you wil automatically make use of the Page
layout that is stored in the 1512 System disk.
This is why it can be useful to keep more than
one such disk, since you can then change from
one page layout to another without all the fuss
of using the menus. Making such changes is very

■ SECTION 23
Word-processing settings

The Change settings menu allows a number of other possible changes, and it's time now to look at some of these. The first item on the Change settings menu is 'Word-processing settings', which affect the way that you work with text as you are typing.

Select this option by moving the shaded bar and pressing RETURN. You will then see the menu of options:

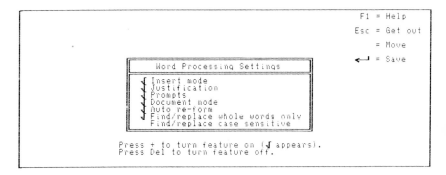

- ■ The **standard settings** that are switched on are indicated by ticks. To switch off, place the shaded band over an option and press the Del key. To switch on an option, place the shaded band over the option and press the + key (either one).

- ■ **Insert mode** means that when you place the cursor over a character and then type another character, the new character will be inserted to the left of the old one, and the cursor will still be over the original character. If you cancel this option, each character you type will replace the character under the cursor, and the cursor moves right at each keystroke. This can make editing very difficult for most purposes. You can, however, turn this effect on or off by using the Ins key.

- ■ **Justification** is normally off. It means that the right-hand edge of the text will be lined up as well as the left-hand edge, and selecting this option will make text-like letters look very neat:

58

The construction of the IC follows normal techniques that are also used for silicon transistors, that is epitaxial deposition and the use of oxidation and etching. The process of epitaxy uses semiconductor material in vapour form. When this condenses on to solid crystal semiconductor, it adds the the cyrstal, atom by atom, with no discontinuity. This perfectly fulfils the requirements for making semiconductor junctions, and allows the junctions to be much more sharply defined than is possible when crystals are grown from molten material.

Note: do not use justification for manuscript that is to be delivered to publishers, because the use of justification makes print estimation very difficult. The exception is, as usual, desktop publishing.

■ The **prompts** option provides full help during text editing. Switch this off only when you are fully familiar with WordStar 1512. You will then be able to work faster.

■ **Document mode** should be used for all normal purposes. You need to change this only when creating instruction files for MailList,(see Part 7).

■ **Auto reform** means that the text you type will automatically be shown on screen as it will appear on paper, following the Page layout that you have specified. This should be turned off only if you intend to alter margins in the middle of text. You will then have to reform text paragraph by paragraph, using the Paragraph reform option from the Editing menu (press F2 key).

■ **Find/replace whole words only** and **Find/replace case sensitive** are options that will be discussed fully later. It's useful to turn on the 'Find/replace whole words only' option.

■ SECTION 24
Printer choice

If you use more than one printer with your PC1512, then another option in the Change settings menu will be useful. This is the SET UP PRINTERS menu. As usual, you need to move the shaded band to this choice. You should then place the PRINTING disk into drive A, and press RETURN. If you forget to change disks, you will be reminded.

■ You will be asked then to make use of the PRINTERS disk from the original set of WordStar 1512 disks. If, as advised, you have made a copy of this disk, use the copy. If you have a twin-drive, you will be asked to put this disk into drive B.

■ You are then asked to choose a printer menu, from a list of three. When you first make use of this, you will see the Amstrad DMP 3000 as the first printer choice, the printer that you specified during installation as second, and 'Printer 3' as third choice. Place the shaded band over the printer you want to change, usually 1 or 3, and press RETURN.

■ You will now see the long list (7 screen pages) of printers that are supported by WordStar 1512. You can change pages by using the PgDn and PgUp keys, and move the cursor in the usual way. Make the choice and press RETURN.

■ The data for the chosen printer is then transferred to your normal working PRINTER disk. If you are using a single drive, this will involve some swapping of disks. Put the original (or copy) PRINTING disk away safely after use.

■ You are then asked to insert your 1512 System disk into drive A. Do so, and press RETURN. This records your printer needs for all future occasions.

■ The example below shows sample text printed with an Epson RX80, using single-line spacing. The point of specifying printers is to record the special printer codes for such effects as underlining, boldface and so on. Each printer uses different codes, so it's only by keeping a record of such codes that WordStar 1512 can cope with changes from one printer to another.

■ Note that double spacing has been switched off!

SECTION 24
Printer choice

This has been typed in A5 format, with **double** line spacing used. The Page layout menu needed for working with the size of paper, but no <u>changes</u> have been made to the Printer setup, so that pages will be printed to the correct size, but the feeding will be incorrect.

The aim of using the Page layout for A5 is to ensure that the correct page breaks are shown, and that the margins are set automatically without any need to use the Margin & Tab menu. You can still use the Margin and Tab. menu to change to other settings for a document or part of a document, but each time you create a new document, or edit this one, you will automatically make use of the Page layout that is stored in the 1512 System disk. This is why it can be useful to keep more than one such disk, since you can then change from one page layout to another without all the fuss of using the menus. Making such changes is very time-consuming, and you would not want to do so if you constantly had to change paper sizes.

■ SECTION 25
Customising the printer

The last option in the Change settings menu allows you to *customise printers*. This means that you can take advantage of all the features that a printer allows in the way of different text styles and sizes, and the printing of special characters, possibly also coloured type. You choose this option by placing the shaded band over it and pressing RETURN.

You will be asked to insert your PRINTING disk, meaning the disk from the working set, not the original printing disk. Once again, you will be given the list of three printers so that you can choose which one to customise. You need to repeat all of these steps for each printer.

■ When you select a printer, you will see a menu of the features of that printer. The example shows the menu for the EPSON X-80:

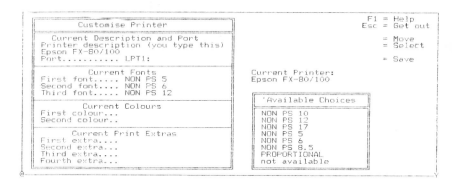

■ **Font**, in this context, means print size and style. The numbers refer to the characters per inch, and if the shaded band is over the first font choice, you will see the range of options in the table on the right.

Customising the printer

■ This particular printer allows a choice of six character sizes. You can make use of only three at a time, the list shown as **Current Fonts**. You might want to change the second font to 5 to allow for large headings, and possibly the first font to 12 if you want to work with A5 paper. Remember, however, that working with fonts other than 10 will mean that the lengths of lines on paper will not be the same as on the screen. They will be the same in terms of character number, but the character size will no longer be 0.1 inch.

■ Each font of this particular printer is described as NON-PS. This means *not proportional spacing*. The letters of the alphabet are not of equal width (compare 'm' with 'i', for example), and machines that allocate the same width to each letter (like typewriters and many printers) give a rather inferior text appearance.

■ Proportional spacing printers allocate spacings between characters that are geared to the width of the characters, so that the number of characters per inch is no longer fixed. Such printers (the Juki 6100 is one) can give very pleasing text, but cause difficulties in the word-processing program because of the variable number of characters per inch. This is why the use of PS will have to be specified here if the printer permits it.

■ Choices in this menu are made by placing the shaded band over a **Current Font**, then pressing the right-arrow key. The band then moves to the first of the **Available choices**, and you can move the band to whatever you want. As you move the band, you will see the **Current font** item change. The change is fixed when you use the left-arrow key to move back.

■ The fonts are obtained when you are entering or editing text, by using the **Print styles** choice (using the F2 key). When you press RETURN, you will see the choice of **First**, **Second** and **Third** fonts (among others). Provided your printer allows such choice, you can select a font for your text.

■ You will be asked to place the cursor where you want the new font to start, then press RETURN. The font you have chosen will affect the rest of the text from the cursor position onwards, but not at earlier positions. You can therefore create text with several font changes.

■ SECTION 25
Customising the printer

        This is a section of text that uses the normal Third Font of
the Epson printer. This is the font of 17 pitch, meaning
seventeen characters per inch, and the Page Layout has been set
to the default 65 columns. This means 65 characters of 10-pitch
size.

■   The illustration shows text in 17-pitch font, using the Epson RX-80
    printer. Remember that if you are using a daisywheel printer, your
    only way of changing fonts is to change daisywheels, so that the
    font choices are not relevant.

■ SECTION 26
Print extras

You can opt to have text in more than one colour of print if your printer supports this. In addition, the **Print Extras** portion of the **Customise Printer** menu allows you to make use of any special characters or features of the printer.

■ To make use of **Print Extras**, go to the **Customise Printer** menu as detailed in Section 25, choosing the printer you want to use.

■ Not all printer types will offer any options here. Check what is available by shifting the shaded bar to the **First extra** line, and look at the **Available Choices** list at the right-hand side.

■ The following examples are taken from the menu for the Juki 6100 in order to illustrate this feature. The Juki 6100 allows six choices, listed as CHAR UNDER S1 to CHAR UNDER S6. These are special characters as follows:

CHAR UNDER	Printed shape
S1	¢
S2	⌐
S3	§
S4	£
S5	¨
S6	ç

■ In order to use these characters, you must decide which four of the six available you will need. For the Juki 6100, the most important is usually the English pound sign, CHAR UNDER S4. This is selected by placing the shaded bar over **First extra**, then using the right-arrow key to get on to the **Available choices**. Now move the shaded bar down the list to CHAR UNDER S4, then press the left-arrow key. The **First extra** will now be the pound sign. Other extras can be selected in the same way.

■ When you have made these choices, press RETURN. You will be asked to insert the 1512 System disk again so as to record the changes. Do this and press RETURN.

■ Use the Esc key to return to the opening menu, and so to word processing.

■ To insert a special character into text, you can now make use of the **Print Styles** menu, then select whichever extra you want into the text. This will *not* appear on the screen, only on the printed material.

➤

■ SECTION 26
Print extras

When the Print Extras have been set up, you can make use of your printer more effectively. Most printers, for example, will print the hash (#) rather than the £ sign, even if you have pressed the £ key. This is therefore one very common use of a Print extra. On the Juki, to take just one example, you can also use the § , ¨ , and ç signs. Using these signs in text requires some care, since they do not show on the screen. Their presence is shown on the 'report' space at the left hand side just above the ruler line, however.

■ Note that the screen does *not* show the print extras as characters of *any* kind, and it it easy to overlook them. Your only guide is the 'telltale' report strip on the top left-hand side of the screen, just above the ruler line. This will show the words 'Print extra', and the number, each time the cursor lands on a **Print extra** character. In addition, you will see a message at the top right-hand side to remind you of the previous **Print extra** that you used.

■ SECTION 27
Print options

Printing with WordStar 1512 is always guided by the various set-up steps that we have looked at so far. None of these, however, deals with printing in pages.

WordStar 1512 is set up to print on continuous stationery, but many daisywheel printers make little or no provision for using such stationery. The Juki 6100, for example, uses a roller feed, and a sprocket feed for continuous stationery is an expensive extra.

For many purposes, the use of separate sheets is preferable. Paper is much cheaper in this form, there is a wider choice, and it's easier to arrange for as many carbon copies as you want. In addition, working one page at a time means that if something goes wrong, only one page will be ruined – and it's easy to reprint one page.

To change the print options, select this choice from the Print Menu

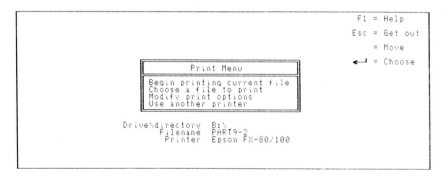

You now see the Print Options menu:

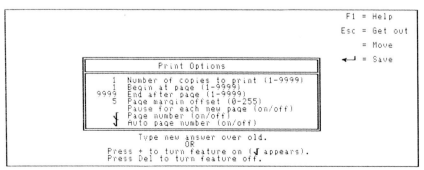

Print options

1 The menu contains several default answers. To replace an existing answer, simply type your own figure over the existing one. The menu allows you to change some quantities that were set up by earlier menus, but these changes will be for this print run only and will not be automatically repeated.

2 You will probably want only one copy of a long document, particularly if you are using carbon paper. For short documents, however, you might want more than one top copy, and you can enter the number into the NUMBER OF COPIES space.

3 The default of starting at Page 1 seldom needs to be changed unless you are printing book chapters, and you want the page numbering to be consecutive. Many authors prefer to give pages temporary numbering (like 2.5), showing chapter number and page number, so as to allow for additions later. Some publishers, however, insist on consecutive numbering throughout the book so that any missing or misplaced pages can be detected.

4 End after page 9999 does not need to be altered if you want to print to the end of the document, only if you want to end printing before the end of the text. Page 9999 is taken to mean the end page of any text.

5 You can alter the page margin offset from the figure that was set up by the PAGE LAYOUT menu.

6 For single-page printing, turn on the PAUSE FOR EACH NEW PAGE feature by pressing the + key when the shaded bar is over this position. The printer will then roll out each page and printing will stop, so that you can feed in the next sheet. Printing will restart when you press any key on the computer.

7 The PAGE NUMBER, and AUTO PAGE NUMBER options allow you to override the choices that you made in the PAGE LAYOUT menu.

PART FOUR

Blocks of text

■ SECTION 28
Block movements

One very important feature of word-processing editing that we haven't looked at so far is block editing. A **block** is a section of continuous text which could be as small as a single character or as large as a whole document. To become a block, the start and finish has to be marked in some way, and when that has been done, the block can be worked with as if it were just a single unit. We have already looked at one aspect of block editing used for deleting a piece of text.

In particular, a block can be separately loaded in from a disk, and it can be deleted, shifted or inserted at will anywhere in the text. Until you have sampled block movements, you haven't really started to appreciate what word processing can do for you.

Take, as an example, the text shown here, an extract from a report in process of construction. This is a straightforward piece of manuscript, which uses the A5 layout that we constructed in the previous Part.

```
        The construction of the IC follows
normal techniques that are also used for
silicon transistors, that is epitaxial
deposition and the use of oxidation and
etching.The whole wafer is subjected to the
processes, so that when the processing has
been completed, the wafer contains a large
number of ICs that have been identically
processed. The good chips in this batch must
then be identified, using equipment that
makes contacts to each chip in turn and spits
red paint on to defective chips. The good
chips are then sliced out and separated off,
and the bad chips are re-melted.
        The process of epitaxy uses semiconductor
material in vapour form. When this condenses
on to solid crystal semiconductor, it adds to
the crystal, atom by atom, with no
discontinuity. This perfectly fulfills the
requirements for making semiconductor
junctions, and allows the junctions to be
much more sharply defined than is possible
when crystals are grown from molten material.
```

■ SECTION 28
Block movements

The report is shown here just as it has been hastily typed. The author has introduced a topic, and then explained it later. Looking over the text, after it has been saved on disk, he realises that it might be better to explain *epitaxy* nearer to the point where the word has been used.

How does he make alterations without retyping? The answer is to move text about in blocks. The main block actions are **Move, Copy** and **Delete**, and all three are available from the **Editing Menu** (press F2 when editing), first page.

1 Shift the shaded bar to the MOVE TEXT option. Press RETURN.

2 You are asked to move the cursor to the beginning of the text you want to move, and then press RETURN. In this example, the cursor is moved to the start of the second paragraph.

3 When you have pressed RETURN, the message at the top of the screen (now in inverse video) asks you to move the cursor to the end of the block you want to move.

4 As you move the cursor, you will see the chosen text being marked – on a monochrome screen, this appears as grey text on a white background.

5 When you reach the end of the text that you want to move and press RETURN, you will be asked to place the cursor at the point where you want the text moved.

6 In this example, the cursor has been placed following the first sentence, and RETURN has been pressed. This causes the marked block to be inserted at this point, and the whole text now reformats, to look as shown overleaf.

Block movements

The construction of the IC follows normal techniques that are also used for silicon transistors, that is epitaxial deposition and the use of oxidation and etching. The process of epitaxy uses semiconductor material in vapour form. When this condenses on to solid crystal semiconductor, it adds to the crystal, atom by atom, with no discontinuity. This perfectly fulfills the requirements for making semiconductor junctions, and allows the junctions to be much more sharply defined than is possible when crystals are grown from molten material. The whole wafer is subjected to the processes, so that when the processing has been completed, the wafer contains a large number of ICs that have been identically processed. The good chips in this batch must then be identified, using equipment that makes contacts to each chip in turn and spits red paint on to defective chips. The good chips are then sliced out and separated off, and the bad chips are re-melted.

7 The text now contains too many topics and consists of one large paragraph. To split the text, move the cursor to the part that starts 'The whole wafer...', and press CTRL-RETURN. This will create a new paragraph. Note that RETURN creates a paragraph when you are typing new text, but you need to use CTRL-RETURN (Ctrl key and RETURN key together) to break existing text into paragraphs.

■ SECTION 28
Block movements

The construction of the IC follows normal techniques that are also used for silicon transistors, that is epitaxial deposition and the use of oxidation and etching. The process of epitaxy uses semiconductor material in vapour form. When this condenses on to solid crystal semiconductor, it adds to the crystal, atom by atom, with no discontinuity. This perfectly fulfills the requirements for making semiconductor junctions, and allows the junctions to be much more sharply defined than is possible when crystals are grown from molten material.

The whole wafer is subjected to the processes, so that when the processing has been completed, the wafer contains a large number of ICs that have been identically processed. The good chips in this batch must then be identified, using equipment that makes contacts to each chip in turn and spits red paint on to defective chips. The good chips are then sliced out and separated off, and the bad chips are re-melted.

■ SECTION 29
Delete and undelete

A block can be deleted by an almost identical method, but using the **Delete text** option from the **Editing** menu (F2 menu).

When you choose to delete text, you will be asked to place the cursor at the start of the block of text that you want to delete, and then press RETURN. You can then move the cursor to the end of the block that you want to delete. As you do so, the text block will be shown in inverse video. When you press RETURN at the end of the block, the block is deleted.

This deletion need not be permanent, provided you do not delete any other block, switch off, or change to another program. You can un-delete or restore whichever block or line of text you *most recently* deleted.

1 Press the F2 key so as to bring up the Editing menu, page 1. Move the shaded bar to 'Restore deleted text', and press RETURN.

2 You will be asked to place the cursor where you want the deleted text to be placed, and then press RETURN.

3 When you press the RETURN key, the 'deleted' text will be restored. This works only within the same document — if you save the document that has had a portion deleted, you cannot restore the deleted material to this or any other document.

4 The provision for restoring a section of document applies also to a line that has been deleted by using Ctrl-Del (see Section 9). As usual, this applies only if this was the most recent deletion, and in the same document.

Note that the method of moving a block deletes the block and pastes it in elsewhere. If you need to copy a block, leaving the original intact, then use the **Copy text** option rather than the **Move text** option.

■ SECTION 30
Copying and saving copy

Copying text is seldom so useful unless you really want to use the text at more than one place in the *same* document. WordStar 1512, unlike most word processors, makes no direct provision for storing a marked section onto the disk so that it can be inserted into another document, or into a file that is another part of the same document. If you need to do this, proceed as follows:

1 Save your text in the usual way by using Esc and pressing RETURN to take the default of saving the text.

2 Now choose the CHOOSE/CREATE A FILE option at the Main menu. When you have pressed RETURN you will see the list of files that exist on the disk – you can use PgDn to see the list continued if the first page is full.

3 Choose a new file name for the portion that you want to save, and type this into the shaded band at the heading of the list.

4 When you press RETURN, you will have a blank editing screen. Press F2 and select Insert file. Press RETURN until you see the file list again. Now select the file name that you have just saved. Press RETURN.

5 Using this file, delete all of the file except the piece you want to copy on to disk. Use the DELETE TEXT option in the Editing menu, page 1.

6 Now save this in the normal way. When you want to use it in another file, you can use the INSERT A FILE option.

Unfortunately, when you mark a piece of text to copy, the marking is deleted whenever a copy is made. This prevents the use of COPY for repeating stock phrases, which is one of its main uses on other word-processing programs.

Another problem is that it's possible to copy a phrase in such a way that it appears outside the normal line boundary. You will then need to move the start of the phrase towards the left hand edge, and you may need to use PARAGRAPH REFORM to achieve correct spacings.

Always check text very carefully after any changes that involve movement, copying, deletion or restoration.

■ SECTION 31
Inserting a file

A particularly useful action during editing is the option to insert text from another file. This allows you to insert text that you may have used before for some other purpose, so that you can greatly reduce the amount of typing that is needed in your current document.

To insert text, use the F2 key to find the second page of the Editing menu, and move the shaded bar to **Insert a file**.

Insert means that the file will be inserted at the current cursor position, and will not replace any text that you are working on.

You *can* change disks before using **Insert file**, so that the file can be inserted from any other disk of text, but this works only with short files.

You will be asked to place the cursor where you want the text inserted, and then press RETURN.

You will then see the usual disk directory display, and you can use the cursor or mouse, along with PgDn and PgUp, to move through the items with the shaded bar. Press RETURN to insert the chosen file.

This is very useful for such items as standard letters (inserting names and addresses) and pieces of standard text as used by lawyers, accountants, estate agents, and others. For much more on this type of technique, you need to use MailList, see Part 7.

The file may have been formatted differently — you may, for example, be inserting an A4 document into an A5 document. This can be dealt with by using Paragraph reform.

You can insert text that has been created by other programs. For example, you may have text that has been created by the COPY command of MS-DOS, by the RPED editor, or by other word processors.

Not all such text is useable. Text produced by the standard versions of WordStar, for example, will have each ending character of a word changed, and WordStar 1512 does not contain any commands for transforming such text.

In general, text from other sources is useful only if it is described as *straight ASCII text*. The professional versions of WordStar describe this as 'non-document mode', and all other word-processing programs either record in this form or make provision for conversion.

■ SECTION 31
Inserting a file

Text from other sources that is in a different format, particularly a different line spacing, may need a considerable effort to convert, and you may have to work on it line by line, using the Del-left key and Paragraph reform.

If you see any marks on the right-hand side of the screen, other than the paragraph mark (), you will need to delete them. Place the cursor at the start of the following line, and press Del-left for each line affected.

Normally, any text to be inserted should first be copied onto the disk that you will use for creating your file.

Corrections

Oddly enough, authors seem to commit more mistakes like mis-spellings, missing letters, and incorrect punctuation marks when using a word processor than they did before word processors became available. Some believe that this is because in days gone by a secretary would have typed the work more professionally, but a contributory factor is the difficulty of working on screen.

It is an undisputed fact that it's much more difficult to spot mistakes on a screen than on a piece of paper. I don't know why this should be so, but it is. The reasonably bright screen display of the PC machine makes life easier — I find that I make fewer mistakes typing with the PC than with my old BBC Micro-based equipment, in which the screen display is very dim.

You should therefore keep the brightness fairly high, look more carefully at text on the screen, and if the work is important and not too long, you should always print a draft copy and proof-read that.

This applies in particular to important letters (job applications, CVs, etc.), rather less to book manuscripts which will in any case be checked by eagle-eyed sub-editors. Articles for magazines should be proofed rather carefully because if deadlines are involved, mistakes may not be picked up at the editing stage.

The move, copy, delete and insert techniques are even more useful in letters and in standard documents than on manuscripts. You can, for example, record a standard letter and a list of names and addresses on a disk. You can then make a copy of this file and edit it, with a name and address inserted into the correct place and the other names and addresses deleted. Printing this file will give a letter to one particular addressee, and the process can be repeated as often as you like.

An improvement is to keep the standard letter and the name/address list as two separate files, and insert both into a temporary file when needed. This removes the risk of saving back a mutilated file of the standard letter or name list. This, however, is really much better handled by the accompanying MailList program, dealt with in Part 7.

File management

Unfortunately, WordStar 1512 makes no provision for 'locking' any file so that it can't be written over and replaced by editing, so that you have to be careful about this.

When you make a new version of a file, the older version is retained temporarily on the disk, with a .BAK extension name. If you have changed a file in a way that you subsequently regret, you can recover the .BAK file version, but the method is not straightforward.

1 You are not allowed to choose for editing any file that has the extension letters BAK or $$$. This is a safeguard to prevent you from carelessly editing files that you might want to keep unchanged.

2 To recover such a file, you need to rename it, using some other extension letters, such as TXT.

3 You will need to go to the file management menu. Use the Esc key as many times as is necessary to get to the opening Menu, and then move the shaded bar to FILE MANAGMENT, and press RETURN.

4 You will be asked to insert the 1512 System disk into drive A, and press RETURN.

5 The options that you have in this menu are COPY, MOVE, RENAME or DELETE – all applying to recorded files on the current disk. Choose the RENAME option.

6 You will see your directory of files (single drive users will be prompted to change disks). Move the shaded band to select the file with the BAK extension.

7 You will be asked to type a complete new filename, and press RETURN. When you see the new name in the list, press Esc. This takes you back to the file management menu, and you can carry out any other Copy, Move, Delete or Rename actions now. Press Esc again to get back to Word processing.

8 You can now make use of the renamed file as you wish. Note, however, that the .BAK version no longer exists. If you want to keep the old version, start a new file under a different name, and insert the old file into this in order to make changes. In this way, the older file wil be retained, and you will also have a new version.

➤

■ SECTION 33
File management

My own preference is to keep all important files on a disk that is write-protected, so that nothing can be written back on to the disk. If it took you several weeks to type all the data into one disk set of files, you'll want to ensure that it remains safe. You can then make use of such files by inserting into a new file as needed.

■ SECTION 34
Find and replace

Two actions that are essential to word processing are the **Find** and **Replace** facilities. These allow you to find a particular word or phrase in a piece of text, and to shift the cursor there. Alternatively, you can find a word or phrase, and replace it with another word or phrase. If the word or phrase occurs several times in the text, you can choose global search and replace, which means that occurrence of the word/phrase will be found and the replacement carried out. An alternative is selective replacement, in which each find action causes a pause until you signal that you want the replacement carried out or not.

A memo example .
        At this stage, an example of the type of
work   that can be achieved with only the most
elementary   commands of Pocket WordStar   will
be   useful.   At   the   same   time,   I   want   to
introduce   another very useful   feature,   the
dot   command   that will be   used   extensively
later. The object of the exercise is a simple
memo,   which will in almost every respect use
the defaults of the system. The one exception
is page numbering.   We don't normally need to
number   that   pages   of   a   memo   because   by
definition,   a   memo should consist of only a
page   or   part-page.   Page   numbering   is   a
default in Pocket WordStar,   however,   and we
need some positive action to turn it off. The
command   to do this must be included   in   the
text   itself,   and   its form is numbering   on
again. The important point about this type of
command   is that it is permanently placed   in
the text,   can be seen on the screen,   but is
not   normally   printed.   The   dot   coming
immediately   before a letter is the signal to
the   machine that this is a   command,   to   be
obeyed   but not printed.   Such a command must
normally be put in a line of its own and   not
mixed   with   ordinary text.   The dot must   be
placed   on the first column,   no matter   what
setting you have used for the left margin.

■ SECTION 34
Find and replace

To see this in action, make sure that you have a suitable file in the machine. The example below is part of a first draft of a book on Pocket WordStar for the PCW machines, using text recorded on a BBC computer.

We can now search for the word 'default'. This is done by pressing the F2 key so as to get to Editing menu 2. Now move the shaded bar to **Find and replace** and press RETURN.

You will be prompted at the top of the screen to type the word(s) you are looking for. There is space to type 30 characters. For our example, type the word **default** and press RETURN.

When you have typed this and pressed RETURN, the next prompt, **Replace** (+ / −)?, will appear. When you are using this command only to *find* text, you should press the - key (either one). This leaves no mark on the screen — the shaded block stays where it is.

Pressing RETURN will now cause the word 'default' to be found, and flashed for your attention.

1 You now have two options. You can press Esc to indicate that finding this first occurrence of the word or phrase is sufficient.

2 The flashing will now stop, and the cursor will be positioned just following the last character of the word or phrase.

3 The alternative is to search for the next occurrence of the word or phrase. To do this, press RETURN. Try this, specifying the word MEMO this time in the example.

4 Each time the word is found, it is flashed, and you have the options of pressing Esc to leave the cursor at that point, or RETURN to find the next occurrrence.

5 When the word can no longer be found, you will get a message in the centre of the screen, and you can press Esc to get back to your text. The cursor will be left at the end of the last word/phrase which was found.

■ SECTION 34
Find and replace

The FIND action operates from the cursor position forward through the text, so that if you are at the end of the text, you need to move the cursor to the start again before trying to find a word or phrase.

The option that allows you to ignore the case of letters is very useful if the word might occur either at the start of a sentence or otherwise in capital letters in the text. This is the default, and if you do not want to use it, you will have to select the **Find/replace case-sensitive** option in the Word processing settings menu (see Section 23).

In addition, you may already have selected the **Whole words only** option for Find/replace in the Word processing settings menu. This will mean that the word **memorandum** which occurs in the text, will *not* be flashed. If you want to be able to find words embedded in others, then this option will have to be altered, see Section 23.

You do not need to type the wanted material again if you need to carry out another search, because the word that you have typed in the Find box remains there until you type another word or phrase.

■ SECTION 35
Exchange

Exchanging, or find-and-replace, is an action that needs to be carried out with more care. The action is started in the same way as a Find action, and the crucial difference is that you need to type a +, using either + key, when you are prompted by **Replace** (+ / −)?. When you press the + key at this point, a tick is shown alongside the prompt, and you will now be ready for word replacement unless you press the Esc key.

Following the example text, you now proceed as follows, if the word memo is to be replaced by the full word **memorandum**.

1 Select the FIND AND REPLACE option. If you have kept the text that you used in the previous section, you will not have to type the word memo again, because it will be in place.

2 You can proceed to the next step by pressing RETURN, or using the down-arrow key. Press the + key to indicate that you want to replace the found word(s).

3 Press RETURN or down-arrow. You will now be prompted to type replacement text. Once again, you can type up to 30 characters.

4 Press RETURN or down-arrow after typing the replacement.

5 You are now asked about AUTOMATIC REPLACEMENT. If you type + here, each and every occurrence of MEMO will be replaced by MEMORANDUM. This is the usual application of the replacing action.

6 If you do not type a +, then replacement is not automatic. Each time the word MEMO is found, you will see a menu that offers you the choice of REPLACE (the default) or SKIP. You will have to move the shaded bar if you want to skip a replacement. Whatever you choose (Skip or Replace) will be the default choice next time the menu appears.

7 The Find & Replace action continues until the end of the document (unless you press Esc), with no messages, and the cursor will be left at the end of the file. If automatic replacement has been specified, then you will see only brief flashes as each occurence of the found word/phrase is replaced, and you will know when the process has ended when you see the cursor at the end of the file.

If you have replaced a word with one of a very different length, then you may have to use the **Paragraph Reform** action to make the text fit correctly between the margins.

Warnings

When words are exchanged, the machine does so blindly, and it's possible to make exchanges that will have ridiculous results unless you have specified whole-word replacement. For example, if you exchange each *smith* for *jones*, you may find a word *blackjones* which is new to you and to the dictionary!

This has to be watched in particular when you are correcting some spelling or typing mistakes with a Find & Replace action. Suppose, for example, that you have a bad habit of typing 'will' as 'wil'. You could exchange each 'wil' for 'will' in a document — and then find that each 'will' has become 'willl' as a result, and each 'wilful' has become 'willful'.

The correct method of avoiding this is to make intelligent use of the options, specifying whole word replacement rather than the (default) part-word replacement.

The really dangerous replace actions are these in which you opt for automatic replacement. If you are absolutely certain that global replacement cannot do any harm, you can do so, but *always* check your text carefully afterwards.

The find and replace facilities are extremely useful for actions which would be tedious if you had to type each change. You cannot, unfortunately, incorporate items like underlining into the replacement text. It would be very useful, for example, to be able to replace each occurrence of 'typing' by '**typing**', but WordStar 1512 cannot do this.

Another very common use is to avoid typing certain words. In a book, I might have to type the word 'microprocessor' several hundred times. By abbreviating this to M/, something that would not occur normally in text, I can use a search and replace action to replace each M/ by microprocessor.

This should not be done to excess, otherwise there is a risk that you will lose track of your abbreviations, unless you keep a note of them, perhaps in a file. One considerable advantage of using search and replace is consistency. If you replace each M/ by microprocessor, you need spell 'microprocessor' correctly only the one time. This avoids typing errors that can occur when you are constantly typing the same word over and over again.

One warning is needed here, particularly for book authors. The use of Find and Replace is something that tempts you to work with large pieces of text, so that all the work can be done in one effort. You will normally work

▶

■ SECTION 36
Warnings

in Chapters, but it's better still to work in shorter sections, perhaps half or even quarter-chapters. This allows you to work with shorter documents.

This is a considerable advantage with WordStar 1512, particularly if you need to search around a document a lot. This action can be slow, and the longer the document, the slower it becomes. When you rework a document, it's a good idea to create a new document, with a new title (CHAP6C.003 for example) for each revision.

This is because you will be replacing the previous version each time. The previous version then becomes a .BAK file, which can be recovered, but the version before that is gone for ever. You can, of course, read a .BAK file into your current file by renaming it, and if you like to rework your text a lot, it's as well to use different file names each time.

When you create, for example, CHAP6B.003, you can start by inserting the text from CHAP6B.002, or from CHAP6B.001 as you choose, depending on how you want to rework the text. When each chapter section has reached its final version, you can join the sections by placing all the sections in order into a new file. This will be the final section file, and you can then carry out any finishing touches (like exchanging 'polygonal' for 'many-sided') on this one. Of course you might like to follow the example of Oscar Wilde who, asked what he had done that morning, said that he had put in a comma. When asked what he would do in the afternoon he said: ''Take it out again''.

PART FIVE

More advanced work

Tables and columns

The straightforward use of WordStar 1512 is comparatively simple, and the use of the menus and Help sections will keep you on the right lines. When you need to carry out more complicated work, however, many problems can arise that can appear to be very puzzling. In this section, we shall deal with some of these problems and their solutions. The first of these is working with columns.

For many types of text, you need to deal with columns of numbers or words, such as you might meet in listing the default settings of Page Layout, for example. Unfortunately, the setting of work in columns is easy only if you are not going to make any changes.

	Columns	Example	
Letter	Code	Letter	Code
A	65	N	78
B	66	O	79
C	67	P	80
D	68	Q	81
E	69	R	82

This type of table, which makes use of the TAB stops and spacebar, can be entered, saved, and printed with no problems.

■ SECTION 37
Tables and columns

For more elaborate work, it's better to set the margins and tab stops to suit the table.

1 To do this, space down a couple of lines, and then enter a line of your table as you would want to see it, using the spacebar and the delete keys to get the spacing as you would want it.

2 Now use the F2 key to get to the MARGINS AND TABS menu. Delete the old tab settings, and put a tab stop at the start of each column in your sample line.

3 Leave the margins and tabs setting menu, and return to the text. Space up, and enter your titles, using the new tab stops.

4 Space down and enter the rest of the table, using the tab key only for spacing and pressing RETURN at the end of each line.

```
              More Columns
No.       Surname      Forename      Age   Sex
001       Pottersbar   Dennis        24    M
007       Watford      Bill          32    M
012       Frogmore     Sheila        27    F
013       Hitchin      Jim           34    M
015       Ware         Stella B.     59    F
016       Ware         Perival       62    M
018       Age          Steven        46    M
```

Problems start if you need to edit a line, or if you start using the spacebar or deleting spaces. The usual problem is that the auto-reformatting action will prevent the items from being put into the correct places. With perseverance, it is often possible to make minor changes without too much bother.

■ SECTION 37
Tables and columns

If your work consists almost entirely of tables, and these will need much editing, then it makes life much easier if you turn off the automatic reformatting. Unfortunately, WordStar 1512 offers no temporary method of doing this.

1 To turn off automatic formatting, get to the Opening menu, and choose the CHANGE SETTINGS menu.

2 From this menu, choose WORD PROCESSING settings.

3 Move the shaded bar to AUTO RE-FORM and press the DEL key.

4 Press RETURN, and then return to Word processing by pressing Esc until you have your text again.

5 You will now be able to edit tables as you please, with no effects on the formatting of the table. If you need to reformat a paragraph of ordinary text, you can do so with the PARAGRAPH REFORM option of the Editing menu.

■ SECTION 38
Foreign characters

In the course of many types of work, you may have to make use of characters that are accented. These letters occur in French, Spanish, German and many other European languages, and if your need for WordStar 1512 includes preparing quotes for export orders or letters overseas, you must be able to include such characters.

Unfortunately, your printer may not be able to cope, even if WordStar 1512 can. There is little point in being able to see such characters on the screen but be unable to print them.

The only point about being able to reproduce the characters on screen alone, then, is that you can record the text and send it by disk. Don't rely on being able to send it by electronic mail, because not all electronic mail systems will cope with the range of code numbers that WordStar 1512 can use for these characters.

The technique for obtaining these characters is as follows:

1 When you need such a character, look up the PC 1512 manual, Appendix 3.1. Look at the range headed 128 to 240 for the accented and Greek characters.

2 You can obtain any character that is in a box by itself, or in the right-hand side of a box that is split to contain two characters.

3 To obtain the character on screen, you need to make use of the number that is printed underneath the character(s).

4 To place a character into text, hold down the Alt key, and type the number using the digits in the keypad at the right-hand side of the keyboard. The digits on the keys at the top of the main keyboard have no effect.

5 When you release the Alt key, you will see the accented character appear.

For example, if you want é, then hold down the Alt key while you type 130 on the keypad. The character will appear when you release the Alt key.

Where a box is split, you cannot obtain the character on the left hand side. For example, typing Alt 187 gives a graphics shape, not the large + sign. Similarly, you cannot obtain the Swedish slashed O by using 157, though you may be able to make do with the Greek phi, 237, in its place.

➤

■ SECTION 38
Foreign characters

As far as printers are concerned, many types of dot-matrix printer will reproduce the characters correctly. Any printer that is described as being compatible with the IBM PC printer should be able to reproduce WordStar 1512 text that contains these accented characters.

If you are using a daisywheel printer, you may be able to cope either by using the Print Extra characters, or by using a different daisywheel that prints the accented characters in place of others like the hash symbol.

■ SECTION 39
Dot commands

A **dot command** is a command that is entered into your text, recorded with it, seen on screen, but not printed. This is a way of forcing certain instructions, particularly to the printer, to be obeyed without the complications of changing page layouts or printer setup.

The name arises because the form of the command is a dot followed by various letters. A dot has been chosen because no known word starts in this way, allowing the dot command to be distinguished from any normal text. In addition, the dot command will be seen in inverse video. If you see a dot command that is *not* in inverse video, then it is misplaced and will not operate correctly.

In addition, the dot of the dot command must be placed in column 1 of the text. If the command starts in any other column, the whole command, including the dot, will be printed but its effect ignored.

One dot command is put in automatically. The **.pa** command is used to signal the end of a page, and it is put into text by the action of the **End page** option from the Editing menu. Other dot commands have to be put in by you as you edit the text.

As well as starting each dot command on column 1, you must take a new line to each dot command by pressing RETURN. These new lines do not appear when the text is printed, because the dot commands cause special codes to be sent to the printer, and the carriage return is not included with these codes.

The dot commands listed in the HELP pages of WordStar 1512 are:

.he   Specify a header phrase for each page of text.

.fo   Specify a footer phrase for each page of text.

.op   Turn off page numbering.

.fi   Include another file in printed text.

.pa   Take a new page.

. .   Comment line, not printed.

.pn   Specify page number following.

A header is any piece of text that is automatically printed at the head of each page, within the top margin. The usual header is a title of some sort, perhaps a Book title and/or Chapter title.

➤

■ SECTION 39
Dot commands

A footer is a piece of text that is printed at the bottom of the bottom margin. This might be a title, but more often is a page number. Since page numbers are dealt with separately, there is no point in using a footer for such a purpose. If the header consists of a Book title, the footer might contain the Chapter number. You can put a page number in a footer by using the character # in the footer, such as Chapter 2.#.

If page numbering is on (the default), it is very cumbersome to have to alter the page layout in order to turn page numbering off. Using a dot command for this purpose allows you to turn page numbering off for letters and similar uses.

Being able to include a file means that a short document can call on others on the same disk when printing. This allows you to split a document into sections, but yet print it as one continuous document.

The comment line allows you to put reminders into your text. These will show on screen when you are editing, but will not be printed on paper. It's a good idea, for example, to have a reminder line each time you include a file with .fi so that you know what this file does.

The .pn command allows you to set a page number from which the normal page numbering will start. This is useful if you print a book in Chapters, but need consecutive page numbering.

There are several dot commands that are not listed in the HELP pages. These include:

.MT   Alters the blank margin at the top of the paper. For example, .MT5 gives a five-line space.

.MB   Gives a bottom margin, such as .MB6. These dot commands are often more useful than altering the Page settings.

.HM   Determines the header margin, the number of lines down from the top of the page at which the header will be printed. Example: .HM1

.FM   Determines the footer margin similarly, like .FM2

.CP   Allows text to be kept together rather than split over a page. For example, .CP5 means that the next five lines will be kept together, so if there are only three lines left on the page, a new page will be taken after the .CP command.

■ SECTION 40
Headers and footers

The use of headers and footers takes a certain amount of care if you are not accustomed to the idea. In particular, getting a header to print just where you want it, and trying to combine a footer title with a page number can be actions that drive the average user to strong language, strong drink or strong actions. In this respect, as in so many others, a molehill of experience is worth a mountain of advice.

To illustrate the uses of headers and footers, then, we shall look at a sample piece of text. This is an extract from the first Chapter of a book about free software, and it carries three dot commands in the first three lines.

The commands can be printed by the simple method of shifting each one from column 1 into column 2, and this allows you to see how the commands look:

```
.he       Public Domain Software
.fo       Chapter 1.
..  Start of text - not Spell checked.
  Chapter 1 .
  Free software .
Nothing in this life is ever free, apart from
the   promises   of politicians, and   we   know,
with  a few exceptions, what these are   worth.
Free   software  will cost you  about   £3   per
disk,   assuming  that  you  supply  the  disk
yourself, and the minimum number of disks per
order   is 3. This is the requirement  of  the
PDSig,  the Public Domain  Software  Interest
Group,  based  in Crowborough,  Sussex  (full
address   given in Appendix. What you pay  for
is   not, however, the software,  because  the
software  is genuinely free. The  payment  is
for  the  cost of copying each disk,  and  to
this  payment will be added a postage  charge
which  will vary depending on how many  disks
are  to be copied. Since the PC type of  disk
is   so common, and particularly easy for  the
group   librarian  to  copy,  you  often  find
bargain offers (like 10 disks for £10,  disks
```

➤

included) of this format appearing in the PDSig journal.

The software, then, is free, and you pay only for the cost of copying, for disks if you do not provide them, and for postage. The big question is, just how much is free software worth? Many computer users who enthusiastically loaded free software along the telephone lines when the service became available for home computers found that the software that they got wasn't good value for money - even when free. If you were one user who became disillusioned with the idea then, take heart, because public domain software for the PC is a very different matter, and couldn't be more different from these amateurish free programs that appeared for the BBC 'B' and other small machines several years ago. The

1 The header command has been typed so that the header will appear at the centre. You CANNOT use the Centre option of the Editing menu for this purpose, because it will shift the dot command as well. Centring is done, therefore, by spacing out after typing the dot command.

2 The footer is typed part of the way along the line, in order to leave room for a page number if we later decide to add a page number with the hash sign, #.

3 The comment line is a reminder to the author — the whole Chapter will be put through a Spellcheck program later — and when this has been done, the reminder line will be changed.

The result of these dot commands can be seen in the sample shown opposite.

Public Domain Software
Free software .

Nothing in this life is ever free, apart from the promises of politicians, and we know, with a few exceptions, what these are worth. Free software will cost you about £3 per disk, assuming that you supply the disk yourself, and the minimum number of disks per order is 3. This is the requirement of the PDSig, the Public Domain Software Interest Group, based in Crowborough, Sussex (full address given in Appendix. What you pay for is not, however, the software, because the software is genuinely free. The payment is for the cost of copying each disk, and to this payment will be added a postage charge which will vary depending on how many disks are to be copied. Since the PC type of disk is so common, and particularly easy for the group librarian to copy, you often find bargain offers (like 10 disks for £10, disks included) of this format appearing in the PDSig journal.

The software, then, is free, and you pay only for the cost of copying, for disks if you do not provide them, and for postage. The big question is, just how much is free software worth? Many computer users who enthusiastically loaded free software along the telephone lines when the service became available for home computers found that the software that they got wasn't good value for money - even when free. If you were one user who became disillusioned with the idea then, take heart, because public domain software for the PC is a very different matter, and couldn't be more different from these amateurish free programs that appeared for the BBC 'B' and other small machines several years ago. The reason is that the operating standard MS-DOS is used only by machines in the 'business' class. This doesn't mean that games or lighter types of

■ SECTION 41
Control of headers and footers

The use of headers and footers with WordStar 1512 seems to allow much less control than most other word-processing programs, particularly other members of the WordStar family. This, however, is only because so many dot commands have been omitted from the HELP pages.

In particular, you might think that you have no control over the lines on which headers and footers appear — they will, by default, always be on the first line and the last line, respectively.

In fact the .HM and .FM dot commands control the position of headers and footers. These have to be used in conjunction with .MT and .MB to control the top and bottom margins, respectively. It's up to us to make sensible use of the numbers that follow the dot commands. There's no point, for example, in specifying a header position of 5 lines with .HM5 if you have specified only 2 lines margin with .MT2.

The use of a footer also cancels the appearance of the page number, which looks like a grave disappointment for any author who likes to have a footer consisting of a Chapter number or name along with a page number. You can, however, put page numbering into a footer by using the # sign.

The example opposite illustrates the use of some of the other dot commands, and the result of using them is shown on page 100.

```
.mt10
.hm2
.fm2
.fo                     Page #
.he Test page
.igthis is not to be printed
.mb4
this is a line
```

that is another

All in triple spacing.

Demonstrating dot commands.

Like .cp10, which ensures that if fewer than

ten lines are left on a page, the following

text will be put on the next page -

```
.cp10
```

Not to be split between pages at any cost,

hence the use of the dot command

■ SECTION 41
Control of headers and footers

Test page

this is a line

that is another.

All in triple spacing.

Demonstrating dot commands.

Like .cp10 which ensures that if fewer than

ten lines are left on a page, the following

text will be put on the next page -

Page 1

- -

Not to be split between pages at any cost,

hence the use of the dot command

■ SECTION 41
Control of headers and footers

Note: you may find when you are using a slow daisywheel printer, that the printing will stop before the end of a page, with a screen message to the effect that the printer is out of paper or off-line. This is usually not the case — the problem is usually caused by the printer buffer.

The printer buffer is memory that is contained (normally) within the printer so that the computer can send text characters to the printer and not be tied up while the printer gets on with printing the text.

Because of the printer buffer, however, there is a comparatively long time between sending each batch of text to the printer. The computer interprets this long time as a fault condition. If you press any key as invited when this message appears, printing will proceed normally.

To prevent this problem, you need to make use of the MODE command of MS-DOS. Details of the steps needed are shown in Appendix 2.

When you make use of headers and footers, it's advisable to take a close look at your page layout to make sure that it is suitable.

For the type of single-spaced text that we have been using, a header of 3 lines is better, because it allows more space between the header and the start of the text. The footer position can be raised by specifying a smaller page length, or by using a .FM type of command.

The page shown here has been laid out for A5, but with a top margin of 3, and a page length of 43. This places the header and the footer into better positions relative to the top and bottom of the page and the rest of the text.

➤

Chapter 1 .
Free software .
Nothing in this life is ever free, apart from the promises of politicians, and we know, with a few exceptions, what these are worth. Free software will cost you about £3 per disk, assuming that you supply the disk yourself, and the minimum number of disks per order is 3. This is the requirement of the PDSig, the Public Domain Software Interest Group, based in Crowborough, Sussex (full address given in Appendix. What you pay for is not, however, the software, because the software is genuinely free. The payment is for the cost of copying each disk, and to this payment will be added a postage charge which will vary depending on how many discs are to be copied. Since the PC type of disc is so common, and particularly easy for the group librarian to copy, you often find bargain offers (like 10 disks for £10, disks included) of this format appearing in the PDSig journal.

The software, then, is free, and you pay only for the cost of copying, for disks if you do not provide them, and for postage. The big question is, just how much is free software worth? Many computer users who enthusiastically loaded free software along the telephone lines when the service became available for home computers found that the software that they got wasn't good value for money - even when free. If you were one user who became disillisioned with the idea then, take heart, because public domain software for the PC is a very different matter, and couldn't

Chapter 1.

■ SECTION 42
File insertion

File insertion into a document by means of the .fi command is a very useful way of combining files and allows you a lot of latitude.

Suppose, for example, that you are typing a piece of work that calls for a table to be included. You might not have the material for the table at hand, so all you need to do is to use a dot command line that calls for the file to be inserted when you are ready to print. This has the very considerable advantage that you do not have to cancel auto-reforming in the middle of a document.

Here's an example of such a document. We can imagine that the file containing the table has not been prepared, but that we shall give it the filename of TABLE. In fact, this is the table that was used earlier in this Part. In addition, the dot command has been shifted one space right so that it appears on the print-out:

```
        In this year, we have had our staff
greatly depleted by natural wastage, in
particular by the setting up of a potato
crisp factory two blocks away.
        Our current staff list is now:

 .fi b:table

- from which you can see that we are down to
the critical number required for continuing
operations, and the Wares are seeking
retirement.
```

The dot command .fi PART5-2 is put in a line of its own, with the dot in column 1. A line is left free on each side so that the table is not placed hard against the rest of the text.

It is VERY important to include the drive letter in the filename when you use the .fi command. If you do not do so, the file *will not be printed*, and only the gap that you have left will appear. The inserted file *must* be on the same disk or on a specified drive, such as the file C:TABLE.

➤

The final printed version should look like this, when the dot command has been moved to its correct position:

```
        In this year, we have had our staff
greatly depleted by natural wastage, in
particular by the setting up of a potato
crisp factory two blocks away.
        Our current staff list is now:

    No.      Surname      Forename   Age Sex

    001      Pottersbar   Dennis      24    M
    007      Watford      Bill        32    M
    012      Frogmore     Sheila      27    F
    013      Hitchin      Jim         34    M
    015      Ware         Stella B.   59    F
    016      Ware         Perival     62    M
    018      Age          Steven      46    M

- from which you can see that we are down to
the critical number required for continuing
operations, and the Wares are seeking
retirement.
```

■ SECTION 43
Print size

The use of printers that permit different print sizes can bring a lot of difficulties to the use of WordStar 1512. The reason is that what you see on screen is geared to the standard 10-pitch type, meaning ten characters per inch along the line.

Other print sizes are available on many printers, and the example below shows a piece of short text which has been printed in the three pitch sizes that are available by default for this printer, the Epson RX- 80.

As you can see, apart from some formatting changes, the text gives the same number of characters per line for each size of print. This means that if you want to work on a document that uses a different size of pitch, you will need to carry out some calculations first.

As an example, we shall show how to construct a document whose main text will be in 17-point, using A5 paper, with a heading that is in 6-point. This sort of thing requires quite a lot of preparation.

1 From the Opening menu, select the CHANGE SETTINGS menu, and from that menu, the CUSTOMISE PRINTER menu.

2 Make the Second font of the current fonts NON PS 6 rather than NON PS 12. Do this by placing the shaded bar over the Second font, pressing the right-arrow key, moving the shaded bar on the Available choices list to NON PS 6, then pressing the left-arrow key.

3 Press RETURN to leave the Customise printer menu. Insert the System disk as requested, and press RETURN again.

4 Now select the PAGE LAYOUT menu. For this example, I have used the Epson printer, so that this choice was made when the printer selection list appeared.

5 Most of each A5 page will be printed in 17-pitch, so that there are 1.7 times as many characters per inch as there would be in 10-pitch. We shall, however, keep the same margins as for A5 to avoid making the page look too full.

➤

This is a section of text that uses the normal First Font of the Epson printer. This is the font of 10 pitch, meaning ten characters per inch, and the Page Layout has been set to the default 65 columns. This means 65 characters of 10-pitch size.

This is a section of text that uses the normal Second Font of the Epson printer. This is the font of 12 pitch, meaning twelve characters per inch, and the Page Layout has been set to the default 65 columns. This means 65 characters of 10-pitch size.

This is a section of text that uses the normal Third Font of the Epson printer. This is the font of 17 pitch, meaning seventeen characters per inch, and the Page Layout has been set to the default 65 columns. This means 65 characters of 10-pitch size.

■ SECTION 43
Print size

6 Set up as shown below. Since the A5 layout that I used for illustration earlier was for the Juki 6100 printer, the default settings are restored for the Epson, so that all of this will have to be reset.

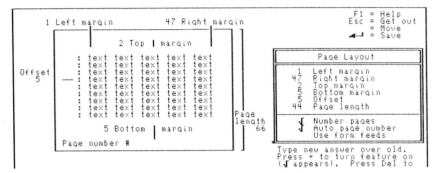

The A5 setting normally has a right margin of 47. This, and the other settings are as for a 10-pitch document because we want to use the normal space on the A5 sheet. If you already have the Page layout set up for A5, steps 4-6 will not be needed.

7 Now return to word processing, and choose a new file name for editing. You will need to set up tabs and margins on this to suit the 17-pitch text.

8 In place of 47 columns, you will need 47 × 1.7 = 79.9 − we'll call it 80. Select the TABS & MARGINS option of the Editing menu, page 2, and move the cursor to column 80, then type R to put in the right margin. You can leave the tabs set at each five columns, because this will be just as useful.

9 You can now enter the text. The tricky bit is to deal with the 6-point text of font 2. This allows only 0.6 of the characters per line, giving 47 × 0.6 = 28.2 (call it 28) characters.

10 The document will start with a title "PRAKTISOFT". This consists of ten letters. Subtract this from 28, to get 18, and take half of this, 9. You need to start this title at column 9.

11 Use the Print styles menu of the Editing menu to select Font 2 in the first line. Use the spacebar to get to column 9, then type PRAKTISOFT. Press RETURN.

➤

107

Print size

12 Use the Print styles menu again to select Font 3, the 17-pitch font. You can now type the rest of the document, using tabs as you require them. It looks better if you start this another line down, to keep it clear of the 6-pitch title.

This shows the text as it looks on the screen:

FRAKISOFT

        This is an illustration of how pitch
sizes can be obtained and mixed in a document
that is intended to be printed with a dot-
matrix printer. An advantage of this type of
printer is the very wide range of styles that
can be used, though you only ever have three
on offer in the Print Styles menu at any one
time. Note that if your text disappears over
the right hand edge of the screen, use the
normal arrowed keys to move the cursor over
to such text.
        You will also find that the text shifts
about violently at the end of each line at
times. This is the auto-reformatting action
in operation, and is quite normal. The most
notable feature of the text, however, is how
it looks on the screen as compared to how it
prints. The heading looks well to the left of
centre on the screen, but because the spaces
were printed in 6-pitch along with the
letters, the printed result is centred.
        Note that if you do this on A4 paper,
you will probably work with a right margin at
about 112 for 17-pitch text. This will mean
that you will have to move the text sideways
in order to read a complete line.

This shows the text as it prints:

FRAKTISOFT

This is an illustration of how pitch sizes can be obtained and mixed in a
document that is intended to be printed with a dot-matrix printer. An advantage
of this type of printer is the very wide range of styles that can be used,
though you only ever have three on offer in the Print Styles menu at any one
time. Note that if your text disappears over the right hand edge of the screen,
you will see an arrow pointing right to indicate that the text exists. You can
use the normal arrowed keys to move the cursor over to such text.

You will also find that the text shifts about violently at the end of each
line at times. This is the auto-reformatting action in operation, and is quite
normal. The most notable feature of the text, however, is how it looks on the
screen as compared to how it prints. The heading looks well to the left of
centre on the screen, but because the spaces were printed in 6-pitch along with
the letters, the printed result is centred.

Note that if you do this on A4 paper, you will probably work with a right
margin at about 112 for 17-pitch text. This will mean that you will have to move
the text sideways in order to read a complete line.

One point to watch is that if you edit this file again, you will find the
margins reset to the normal 47, since this is the setting in the Page layout.
This will make any added or edited text reformat to 47-column width, so
you need to reset the margins before editing any text of this type.

If you want to change to other fonts, you will need to delete the font
change characters. Move the cursor until you see the Font message at the
top left side, and then press the Del key on the keypad. Check carefully
through the text to make sure that no remaining font characters are
embedded in the text. You cannot replace one font character by another;
you have to delete one before you can change to another.

PART SIX

Spellchecking

Outline

There are two main forms of spelling checker available for word processors. One type is loaded into the memory of the computer, and lurks there waiting to be called. When you have typed a word of which you are unsure, you press a pair of keys (such as Alt-P), and the correct spelling will be shown. You can then replace the word you have typed with this spelling.

The second type operates on a complete file, and points out spelling errors to you so that you can do something about it. This is by far a better type to use, because you are not always aware of making spelling errors as you type.

In addition, the second type of spelling checker can find typing mistakes that result in incomplete words (like incoplete, as I typed first time round) and draw these to your attention. Such a checker allows you to type fast and repent at leisure, unlike the first variety which often keeps you at the keyboard for hours. A few checkers combine both methods.

There is also a very useful variation on the second type which will work its way unattended through a document, and present you with a list of errors at the end.

WordStar 1512 uses the second main type of spelling checker, dealing with all the words in a file and asking you to check each mistake as it is pointed out. This is done by using a dictionary of words that comes on a separate disk.

The dictionary is large, but it cannot possibly contain every word you might use, so provision is made for adding words to it, or for creating a specialist dictionary of your own on another disk.

In addition, some words, such as proper names, do not belong in the dictionary, so there has to be some provision for ignoring such words, either once, or each time a word is used in a document.

Sometimes what is typed may not be an obvious mis-spelling. The word 'wil' should probably be 'will', but what should 'ytu' be? The spelling checker will offer suggestions for such cases, and you are free to accept a suggestion, try the next word in the list or the previous one, or type a correction for yourself.

The WordStar 1512 spelling checker requires you to have the document to be checked as the 'current file' that is being edited. This file can be as long or as short as you like, but bear in mind that spell-checking is a lengthy procedure, particularly if a lot of new words are present in the text.

Outline

You have to be *very careful* about adding words to the dictionary. It is quite easy to add words, but if you add a word that turns out to be incorrect, it is not quite so simple to delete it (see Section 64 for details when you have rather more experience with WordStar 1512).

For that reason, you should make a backup copy of the spelling disk, and label it as 'Original dictionary', so that you have at least one copy of the dictionary as it originally was.

Spell-checking always works from the cursor position to the end of the text, so if you want to check a complete document, you need to put the cursor at the beginning. Alternatively, if you want to skip, for example the name and address on a letter, you can do so by placing the cursor at the start of the text you want to work on.

An example

As an example of the spell-checking process, take the (terrible!) piece of text shown here:

```
      This is an exaple of wrok done in a
hurry, a problem that besets all of us at
times at Associated Sludgespewers. Using
WordStar 1512 allows work like this to be
sdone hastily, and then sorted out at leisure
later. Mr Perkins thinks that it might cure
his dyxlexia at last!
```

Type this, and save it under the filename BADSPEL.

1 Now create the new filename GOODSPL, and insert into it the old file BADSPEL.

2 Make sure that the cursor is at the start of this file.

3 Press the F2 key to get Page 2 of the editing menu, and select Spelling correction. DO NOT insert the dictionary disk, Disk 6, into drive A until instructed. Press RETURN when you have done so.

4 The first error found is 'exaple'. The dictionary suggests 'example', and this is correct. Move the shaded bar to CORRECT AS SUGGESTED (if not already there), and press RETURN to make the correction.

5 The next mistake is 'wrok'. Once again, the suggested word is correct, and since the shaded bar is already over the 'Correct as suggested' line, you need only press RETURN.

6 The word 'Sludgespewers' is rather different. This is not a spelling error – the writer has spelled the name of his company correctly – but a name that does not belong in a dictionary. The correct choice this time is IGNORE IN ENTIRE FILE, since that will allow the use of the word in later parts of the document without question provided that it is spelled in the same way.

7 Would you believe that 'WordStar' is not in the dictionary? I added it to mine, and you may want to do the same.

■ SECTION 45
An example

8 The word 'sdone' presents problems. The dictionary cannot recognise this as 'done' with a slipping finger at the start, and looks for other words starting with letter 's'. The correction must be done manually. Select TYPE YOUR CORRECTION, and press RETURN. The Suggestion box clears, and you can now type the correction. When you press RETURN again, you will be asked to Confirm this correction, Replace throughout, Type another correction or Bypass this time. In this case, as in most cases, the first choice is best.

9 The dictionary does not contain 'Perkins', a proper name, so that you can choose IGNORE IN WHOLE FILE, just in case he is referred to again.

10 Finally, 'dyslexia' is incorrectly spelled (!), and the dictionary does not contain this word (well it wouldn't, would it?).

11 At the end of the document, you are asked to press RETURN. Swop disks when prompted, and you will see your corrected document ready to be saved to disk and subsequently printed.

```
        This is an example of work done in a
hurry, a problem that besets all of us at
times at Associated Sludgespewers. Using
WordStar 1512 allows work like this to be
done hastily, and then sorted out at leisure
later. Mr Perkins thinks that it might cure
his dyslexia at last!
```

■ SECTION 46
Dictionaries

Being unable to delete words from the main dictionary is not a severe handicap, provided that all the words have the spelling that you prefer, and it ensures that you cannot corrupt this very large and valuable file.

For some purposes, for example, adding medical or scientific words, you *must* be able to correct, delete and add words. Words that are not in the main dictionary, however, are put in a separate file. This file can be edited, and can even be saved on a separate disk.

If you try to read the *main* dictionary into any form of editor with the idea of making corrections, you will get a message to the effect that any attempt to modify the dictionary will probably destroy the copy altogether. You must *not* therefore attempt to work with the files called \1512\DICTNARY\MAIN.DTY or \1512\DICTNARY\INTERNAL.DTY.

The only file that you can use is the one that is called \1512\DICTNARY\PERSONAL.DCT. Section 64 deals with editing this file so that you can correct dictionary entries that you have made or create a new disk of specialised words.

Other spelling checkers contain an editor that allows you to add or delete words, and to list the words contained in the dictionary. At the time of writing, however, even the cheapest of such checkers was considerably more than that of the whole WordStar 1512 package.

PART SEVEN

Mailing lists

■ SECTION 47
The MailList action

Your version of WordStar 1512 includes a very useful program called MailList, which is intended mainly for creating 'form' letters. Something of this sort comes through my letterbox almost each month:

Mr I. R. Sinclair,
May I call you **Ian**? You see, **Ian**, you are about to become the most privileged householder in **Acacia Avenue**, because you, just you **Ian**, have the chance of entering the **GOLLYGOSH** million pound draw! Think what **Acacia Avenue** would make of your success − and all you have to do, **Ian**, is to send the YES YES I'LL DO ANYTHING label back to us in the reply-paid envelope provided.

Now this letter started life as two sets of documents. One is a letter in which each emphasised word or phrase did not exist − its place was marked by a form of 'stand-in', called a variable. This letter is prepared in the normal way, using the word-processor editor.

The other part of it all is a file, called the Master list, that contains my name and address, split up so that parts, like **Ian** and **Acacia Avenue**, can be picked out as separate lines. This file will also hold similar data for hundreds of thousands of other unfortunate collectors of waste paper. This file has to be prepared using the MailList disk of WordStar 1512.

The two files are then put through a List printer program, which is a type of modified word-processor printer program. This prints the standard letter, and whenever it comes to a 'variable,' it inserts an item from the name/address file.

In this way, hundreds of thousands of letters can be produced with very little human effort, each one looking as if it were an individual production.

We have become so used to this now that we quite automatically throw such letters away. The techniques can, however, be put to useful purposes, particularly if you need to send out lots of letters with a very similar content but individually addressed and with reference to individual needs.

MailList is also very useful for addressing envelopes, printing labels, creating personal telephone directories and many other purposes.

One of the important feaures of MailList is that the file of records (like names and addresses) can be sorted into order in a variety of ways. You can, for example, sort in order of surname, in order of date of birth, or any other type of information.

■ SECTION 47
The MailList action

Using MailList is a matter for experience, and you will not find that the HELP pages of WordStar 1512 are particularly useful to you until you have had some experience. WordStar 1512 provides you with some ready-made data on Disk 5 (Text and Data) to help you in learning these topics.

In the following sections, we'll look at the processes for creating standard letters and other MailList documents **step by step**. This will be easier to follow and more useful for learning purposes than wading through the many HELP pages of MailList. To save constant repetition, I shall describe the process for a twin-disk machine, with the 1512 disks in drive A and a data disk (text and other files) in drive B. If you are using a hard disk machine, the text/files disk will probably be in drive A. If you are using a single drive, you will have to swop disks as and when prompted, and keep the disks very clearly labelled.

■ SECTION 48
Introduction to MailList

A full guide to MailList would take up considerably more space that we could possibly allow for in a book of this size, so that only a reasonable introduction to the use of MailList will be covered here. We shall start with a brief memo, in which three phrases have been represented in a special way, as 'code' names (called 'variable names') surrounded by the ampersand sign (&). These are put at the points where there will be insertions, and the action of MailList is to read the file of names that are to be put in to replace these variable names.

1 Pick a new filename for your Memo, and prepare to edit in the usual way, using the word processing option.

2 Start to write the memo. Following the 'Dear', we shall insert various names, so we want a first name here. YOU DO NOT HAVE TO TYPE THIS.

3 Press the F2 key to get to the Editing menu, Page 2, and select VARIABLE NAMES. This provides all the names that you are allowed to use. The list appears when you press RETURN. Select E FIRST.

4 You will be asked to place the cursor where you want to see the First name appear. You probably have the cursor in place, following 'Dear', so press RETURN. The variable '&first/o&' will automatically be placed in your text.

5 The next variable is needed after the words 'return the', and for this one I have used '&keyword-1/o&', obtained by selecting variable name 's'.

6 The next variable name is '&keyword-2/o&', variable 't'.

7 The memo is now completed and saved on the disk.

Introduction to MailList

```
                        MEMO

Dear &first/o&,

          Much as I hate to ask, could you
please return the &keyword_1/o& I loaned you,
because I want to do some &keyword_2/o& this
weekend.

                    Yours,

                    Bill.
```

You are told in the HELP pages that only the variable names, such as '&first/o&', that are provided by the Editing menu can be used. This is not strictly true, as we shall see later, but it's better to stick to these names as far as possible to avoid complications.

■ SECTION 49
The Master List

The next set of steps is the creation of a file of three words that will be inserted into each memo. To do this, you need to use the Mailing List option from the Opening menu.

1 Select Mailing list, and put in the MailList disk as prompted. When the MailList main menu appears, select CHOOSE/CREATE A MASTER LIST. Type a new filename when the file list appears, using the same data disk as you have saved the MEMO example on. Use a filename such as MEMO.MLD for this list. You must use the extension of.MLD in the name, and you will be prompted if you forget, so that MailList will put it in automatically for you.

2 When the MailList main menu returns, take the first option, BEGIN DATA ENTRY, and press RETURN.

3 You will be presented with a blank form which contains every possible variable name and space for an entry. It helps if you took a note of the names that you used in the memo!

4 Move the cursor down to FIRST, and type a name, such as Jim. Move down by pressing RETURN or the down-arrow key, to Keyword-1, and type 'drill', then to Keyword-2 and type 'drilling'.

5 As you can see, it would have been better to have chosen Note-1 for the activity rather than Keyword-1 – we live and learn. We shall, in fact, make much better use of this form later.

6 After you have typed something for Keyword-2, press PgDn to bring up another record form. Continue until you run out of names, time or patience.

7 When you have entered as many as you want, press Esc. You will see your first 'record' again. A record is a complete set of data for items that will be merged into your text, and each item in the record is a field.

8 Press Esc again to get back to the Main Menu, then again to get to the Opening Menu. Move the bar down to the LIST PRINTING option. Put in the PRINTING disk and press RETURN as requested. You will see a set of options, most of which you do not need at present.

9 Move to PICK PRINT FORMAT and press RETURN. You are given the choice of Letters, Mailing labels, Envelopes, Telephone directory, Proof report, or Rotary cards. Letters are the least specialised of these options.

10 When you pick 'Letters', you will see the directory of your data disk, which should contain both the memo example and the MEMO.MLD file. You are asked to choose a file to print. Pick the filename you used for your memo text.

11 You should now see the MailList Print menu again. You may want to set the PAUSE EACH PAGE option if you are using single sheets of paper.

12 Now select BEGIN PRINTING, and press RETURN

13 After rather a long time, you will see the memos printed (see overleaf). You do not get one memo to each page — they will, in fact, print to the end of the page size that you normally use before you are prompted to feed in another sheet.

If you want each memo to use a new page, then you must end the main memo text with a new-page code, obtained from the Editing menu or by typing .pa in a new line.

The Master List

MEMO

Dear Jim,

      Much as I hate to ask, could you please return the drill I loaned you, because want to do some drilling this weekend.

        Yours,

        Bill.

MEMO

Dear Bob,

      Much as I hate to ask, could you please return the hammer I loaned you, because I want to do some surgery this weekend.

        Yours,

        Bill.

MEMO

Dear Bert,

      Much as I hate to ask, could you please return the chisel I loaned you, because I want to do some woodwork this weekend.

        Yours,

        Bill.

■ SECTION 50
The List files

Carrying out a simple MailList example like the memo example above is straightforward, mainly because when you select List printing at the Opening Menu, the Master List that is already in place is the MEMO.MLD that you created. The Master list, remember, is the list of items that will be put into the standard memo, letter, label or whatever you are using.

When you switch the computer on next time and select List printing, you will probably see that the Master list entry is the default, SAMPLE.MLD. You need to be able to specify which Master list you will use, and this is not possible from the List printing menu.

1 Return to the opening menu, using the Esc key, and select MAILLIST. Press RETURN. You will be prompted to change disks and press RETURN again.

2 This brings up the MailList main menu. Choose the second line CHOOSE/CREATE A MASTER LIST, and press RETURN

3 You will see a listing of all the files on your data disk (single-drive users must change disks as prompted). When you make extensive use of MailList, you will probably keep a disk devoted to such files.

4 Your listing will show two files for each Master list. One will have the extension letters MLD, the other will have the extension MLI. The file you need to specify is the one with the MLD extension (meaning Master List Data). If you select the MLI file, you will get an error message. A Master list file MUST use the MLD extension, and if you omit the MLD letters when you specify a new name for a Master list, you will be prompted and the letters will be added automatically (see Section 51).

5 When you have selected the Master list, such as MEMO.MLD, pressing RETURN will get you back to the MailList main menu. Note that these MLD and MLI files CANNOT be read by the editor of WordStar 1512 unless they are changed to ASCII form. There is provision for this in the Manage Master Lists menu, but you do not normally need to do this.

6 Once you have selected your current Master list using the MailList disk, you can return to the Opening menu to select Word processing or List printing. Any list printing will now make use of the current Master list.

➤

The List files

7 It's often useful to have a copy of your Master list(s), and the List printing menu allows for this by selecting the Print format menu.

8 Choose the PROOF REPORT item, and press RETURN. You will be returned to the MailList Print Menu, with the shaded band on BEGIN PRINTING. Press RETURN to activate this, with paper ready in the printer. Don't forget to modify the print options to allow for pausing at each page if you need to.

9 The proof report shows each record in the form that you see it on screen, even if only part of a record is used.

For a Master list with a very large number of entries, a full proof report is a very large document. Another option obtained from the **MailList print menu** is the second item — **Choose records to print**. This, however is not necessarily useful.

If you select this option, you will find another menu allowing you to print the entire master list, flagged records, or sublists. Printing the entire Master list gives exactly the same printout as the Proof report. Flag letters and sublists are useful only if you have incorporated these items into your Master list. In this example, they have not been used.

Another way of checking the pattern of a Master list on paper is to select the **Test paper alignment** option from the MailList print menu. This prints out a blank Master list form, with letters xxx representing spaces for characters. The HELP screen for this action states that a test pattern is printed, but only the first record in the list. You will probably find that a blank Proof record is printed for each item in your list, so you will probably want to interrupt the printing after one sheet has been printed.

To print just one page of Master list record, use the **Modify print options** option, and select End after page 1.

PROOF REPORT

Record: 00001
Name: Jim
Title:
Company:
Address-1:
Address-2:
Town/county:
Country:
Keyword-1: drill
Keyword-2: drilling
Keyword-3:

Flag:

Date:
Mr/Ms:
Phone-1:
Phone-2:

Note-1:
Note-2:
Note-3:

Record: 00002
Name: Bob
Title:
Company:
Address-1:
Address-2:
Town/county:
Country:
Keyword-1: hammer
Keyword-2: surgery
Keyword-3:

Flag:

Date:
Mr/Ms:
Phone-1:
Phone-2:

Note-1:
Note-2:
Note-3:

Envelopes

Addressing envelopes is an office chore that is extremely tedious, and which can be completely automated by using MailList. Your Master list for envelopes consists of a set of names and addresses, and when you make use of the list in the List printing action, you can specify the use of envelopes.

For envelope addressing, there is no need to use any word-processor file, only the Master list, so that the action is simpler, with no text to insert. For an example, proceed as follows:

1 Use the Esc key as often as is needed to return to the Opening menu, then select MailList. Insert the MailList disk as directed, and press RETURN to get to the MailList main menu.

2 Select the second item, CHOOSE/CREATE A MASTER FILE. This will be the name/address list for your envelopes.

3 You will see the familiar list of files. Type a name, such as ENVELOPE, and press RETURN. You will be asked if you want to create a new master list. Press RETURN to acknowledge. If you typed ENVELOPE (not ENVELOPE.MLD) you will be asked to press RETURN again to add this extension automatically.

4 You will then see the MailList main menu return, with the shaded bar over BEGIN DATA ENTRY. The filename is repeated below the menu box.

5 Press RETURN to start data entry into this list. The same entry form is used no matter what list you happen to be creating. If you want to be able to print your first record independently of others, type a letter in the 'Flag' position.

6 Fill in as many records as you want. You can leave some parts blank, and the blanks need not be in the same places on different records. The Mr/Ms box is not used for envelope addresses, so that whatever you put in here is not printed on the envelope.

7 The same applies to other parts of the record that are not an address, so your address list can contain other information as well, to be used for other purposes. In most cases, the more information you can put on such a list the better, since this makes it more useful. REMEMBER, HOWEVER, THAT YOU MAY BE OBLIGED TO REGISTER UNDER THE 1985 DATA PROTECTION ACT IF YOUR FILES CONTAIN EVEN MILDLY CONFIDENTIAL INFORMATION. No-one really understands this very unsatisfactory piece of legislation, but it seems to apply even to home-computer uses, like Christmas lists. Consult a solicitor if in doubt, and remember that he/she also may be in doubt.

8 Press Esc to end entry. You will then see your first record again so that you can edit it (did you put commas in the correct places, or do you need to remove them ?). When you have edited all the records (use PgDn to get to the next record, even if you have not moved the cursor on the current record), press Esc to return to the MailList main menu.

9 Now use Esc again to get to the main menu.

You can now make use of your Envelopes Master list for printing names and addresses on envelopes. Select the List printing option on the Opening menu, and insert the PRINTING disk as requested.

1 Move the shaded bar to PICK PRINT FORMAT, press RETURN. Select ENVELOPES from the list.

2 At the menu again, select Print options. Move the bar to PAUSE FOR EACH NEW PAGE and press the + key (either + key). This will be needed unless you are using envelopes that are attached to a continuous guide sheet.

3 You can now begin printing. No matter how much data you have put on to your Master list, only the name and address will be used on the envelopes. On the examples below, produced with the Juki 6100, the printing starts 3.5 inches from the left-hand side of the paper. This is suitable for office-size envelopes.

4 If you are using domestic-size C6 envelopes, put the left hand edge of the envelope 1.5 inches in from the printer left-hand side zero mark. This will give a better position for the address.

Envelopes

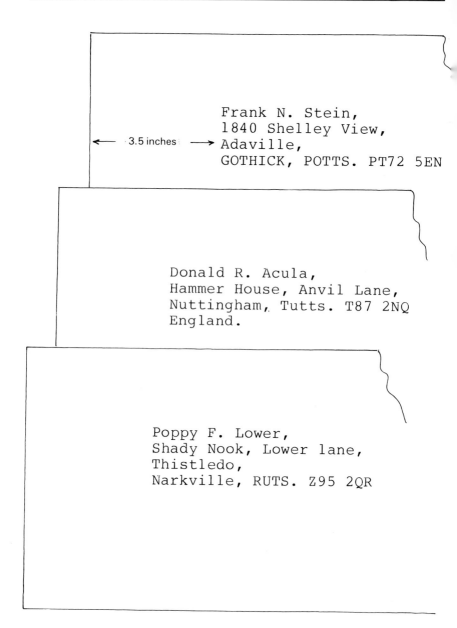

Frank N. Stein,
1840 Shelley View,
Adaville,
GOTHICK, POTTS. PT72 5EN

←— 3.5 inches —→

Donald R. Acula,
Hammer House, Anvil Lane,
Nuttingham, Tutts. T87 2NQ
England.

Poppy F. Lower,
Shady Nook, Lower lane,
Thistledo,
Narkville, RUTS. Z95 2QR

■ SECTION 52
Sorting

Remember that you can specify more than one copy of each envelope or any other MailList document.

You can also order printing to be in an order other than the 1, 2, 3,... order of the records. No matter what the order of the records happens to be (and they, too, can be sorted), you can specify a print order.

1 Get to the MailList print menu. Move the shaded bar down to SORT ORDER FOR PRINTING. Press RETURN.

2 You will see the list of possible sort orders:

Record number
Date
Name
Company
Country/town
Post code
Phone-1
1st keyword
2nd keyword
3rd keyword
Flag

This allows you a very wide range.

3 To illustrate this, select NAME. When you press RETURN, you will be ready to Begin printing. Load in paper, and press RETURN.

4 When the names and addresses are printed this time, after a long delay for sorting, you will see them in alphabetical order of surname.

➤

Donald R. Acula,
Hammer House, Anvil Lane,
Nuttingham, Tutts. T87 2NQ
England.

Poppy F. Lower,
Shady Nook, Lower lane,
Thistledo,
Narkville, RUTS. Z95 2QR

Frank N. Stein,
1840 Shelley View,
Adaville,
GOTHICK, POTTS. PT72 5EN

■ SECTION 53
Mailing labels

When you use the **Pick print format** option from the MailList Print menu, you will also find the **Mailing labels** option.

In many ways, this is much more flexible than the **Envelopes** option, and you will probably find it very useful for envelopes.

The Mailing labels option assumes that you are using self-adhesive labels on a sprocketted roll, and the formats are geared to this. The standard formats are shown on screen when you specify Mailing labels.

Not all daisywheel printers come with sprocket-feed, and this may be an expensive extra. You can use labels on plain paper, one page at a time, but this needs more care. In addition, you will have to cut the rolls of labels into A4 sheets (or some such convenient size). A printer with roller-feed cannot keep paper positioned precisely enough for label printing from a large roll, which is why sprocket-feed (also called tractor-feed) is assumed.

The label sizes and positions on the page must correspond to the type shown on screen. If in doubt, go for the medium size 1-across type. Always specify a pause if you are using hand-fed sheets, and remember to set the Page size option to suit.

If you pick the small label, what you get is shown overleaf, as printed on an ordinary A4 sheet for the name/address list. The printer has paused at each name/address, and the printing is hard against the left hand side of the paper. The spacing between labels is set automatically.

Picking the medium label size gives the same effect — you should use the medium size label only if you need long lines, or if your printer is set up for large print sizes.

If you pick the 4-across format, you have to be sure that your names/addresses will fit. Your printer will also need to be able to cope with 14-inch wide paper.

➤

Mailing labels

```
Frank N. Stein,
1840 Shelley View,
Adaville,
GOTHICK, POTTS. PT72 5EN




Donald R. Acula,
Hammer House, Anvil Lane,
Nuttingham, Tutts. T87 2NQ
England.




Poppy F. Lower,
Shady Nook, Lower lane,
Thistledo,
Narkville, RUTS. Z95 2QR
```

A safer option is the smaller 2-across (shown opposite). If you have specified a pause, then the pause will be after two labels instead of at each label. It would be much better if the pause were at the end of a page, but no provision has been made for this.

Donald R. Acula,
Hammer House, Anvil Lane,
Nuttingham, Tutts. T87 2NQ

Frank N. Stein,
1840 Shelley View,
Adaville,
GOTHICK, POTTS. PT72 5EN

■ SECTION 54
Renaming a file

The advantage of keeping a full record on each name in your Master list is that it enables so much more to be done. In this section, we'll illustrate the setting up of a more extended record, using the short list of names in the ENVELOPES file.

Normally this would be a file of some name other than ENVELOPES, so we'll edit it and rename it as PEOPLE.MLD. You need to get back to the opening menu, specify MailList, and put in the MailList disk as requested.

Select to choose a master list, and pick ENVELOPE.MLD. When the menu returns, pick Begin Data entry. You can now edit your existing records.

Fill in full details on each record, so that you have something like that shown opposite.

This has been selected by using the Flag x that was put in during editing. The page numbering has been turned off and a pause before each page put in, all with the **Print options** menu. Note that turning off the page numbering does not prevent the numbering of the record page.

Now that we know what we have in the file, we can rename it. Return to the opening menu, and pick **File management**. This requires the use of the 1512 System disk.

1 At the File Management menu, choose RENAME.

2 You will be asked to choose a file to rename from the directory of the data disk. Pick ENVELOPES.MLD, and rename to PEOPLE.MLD. Then rename ENVELOPE.MLI to PEOPLE.MLI. It is IMPORTANT to rename BOTH files!

3 You can then return to the Opening menu to choose your next step. In this case, we shall look at the Telephone directory facility.

PROOF REPORT

```
Record:     00001                          Flag: x
  Name:     Frank N. Stein,
 Title:                              Date: 07-01-87
Company:    Spiderweb productions  Mr/Ms: Mr.
Address-1:  1840 Shelley View,    Phone-1: 099-1234-759
Address-2:  Adaville,             Phone-2:
Town/county: GOTHICK, POTTS. PT72 5EN
Country:
Keyword-1:  Work     Note-1: Web spinner, brain surgeon
Keyword-2:  Hobbies  Note-2: Creative biology, computing
Keyword-3:  Car(s)   Note-3: Owns '67 Stashmobile
```

■ SECTION 55
Telephone directory

The telephone directory format of MailList consists of three columns containing the record number, name and telephone number for the subject of each record. To print this directory, proceed as follows:

1 Make sure that the current Master list file is the one you want to use. If in doubt, enter MailList, and use the CREATE/CHOOSE MASTER LIST option to choose the file, in this case PEOPLE.MLD.

2 Go back to the Opening menu, and select List printing. From the Print menu, select PICK PRINT FORMAT.

3 From this menu, pick TELEPHONE DIRECTORY. When you press RETURN, you will be returned to the Print menu. If you were using an extended list, you might like to cancel page numbering (though it is not, in fact, cancelled!) and enable page pause from the Print options menu.

4 When you press RETURN on the BEGIN PRINTING instruction, there is the usual frantic disk activity, and the telephone directory list is printed. Note how the superfluous commas in the Master list are gathered together.

TELEPHONE DIRECTORY


```
00001   Stein,,  Frank N.         099-1234-759
00002   Acula,,  Donald R.        087-2414-599
00003   Lower,,  Poppy F.         092-7162-544
```

A telephone directory needs better organisation than this, so this is a good case for printing with some sorting. The most obvious sorting for such a file is alphabetical by name.

■ SECTION 55
Telephone directory

In the following example, we are assuming that the Master list file is correct and that the type of printout is still specified as Telephone directory. If you have made changes, you will need to return to this format.

1 At the MailList Print Menu, select sort order for printing.

2 Now select NAME from the menu of sort items.

3 Begin printing again when the MailList Print Menu reappears. As before, turning off the page numbering has no effect.

TELEPHONE DIRECTORY

```
00002   Acula,, Donald R.        087-2414-599
00003   Lower,, Poppy F.         092-7162-544
00001   Stein,, Frank N.         099-1234-759
```

There is, unfortunately, no simple method for ensuring that each initial letter gets a page to itself.

You might want a different sorting order for a directory, for example, a list in alphabetical order of company name, of town or post-code. You might even want to list in order of phone numbers, or in some other way using the keywords or the flag letter.

Keywords can be used in many ways. For a file of people for business purposes, you might use one keyword to indicate the type of business (Electronics, Car Sales, Farm spares) and another to indicate more specific details (Capacitors, Mercedes, Massey-Ferguson).

Remember that you cannot sort in order of ANY field. The Note fields cannot be used for sorting, nor the Country, Phone-2, or Address fields. If you want to sort in some kind of address order, use the Post code.

You can incorporate more information into records by making use of **sublists**.

Sublists

A sublist is a set of up to eight extra lines of information that can be added, if wanted, to each record in a Master list. The items in the sublist should be capable of being either applicable or non-applicable.

For example, if a sub-list item is **Christmas box** then this is an item that could be ticked (YES) or left unticked (NO) in each record. This enables the program to find each person on a list to whom a Christmas box should be sent.

You can similarly make use of sublists like Business, Personal, Masons, Alcoholics, Crawlers, Helpful and any other categories you like. Remember that the Data Protection Act gives these people the right to see your files — if you want to keep really confidential information, put it into a card-index

The steps in the creation and use of a sublist can be illustrated on our tiny PEOPLE file.

1 From the MailList main menu, select the MANAGE MASTER LISTS MENU. In this menu, select NAME/RENAME SUBLISTS.

2 You are given a set of eight spaces to type your own sublist titles. Having typed a title, you press the down-arrow key to move to the next line.

3 Press RETURN to end work on the sublist titles. If you forget, and press RETURN too early, you can return to the sublist titles so as to continue entry.

4 Now return to the Manage master lists menu, and select CHOOSE A LIST TO MANAGE, unless you have your list noted as the current list. Select whatever list you want to use with the sublists. In this example, I selected PEOPLE.MLD.

5 Return to the MailList main menu and select the first line, BEGIN DATA ENTRY. This will bring up the first of your records.

6 Press Ctrl-right arrow to get to the sublist menu. This is not noted on the main record, but you can now see a note to the effect that you can return to the main entry form by pressing Ctrl-left arrow.

7 The shaded bar and flashing cursor in the top box invites you to press + to make this record a Business one, or to move to the next box by pressing the down-arrow key. The first record has been marked as Business, Computer-owner.

PROOF REPORT

```
Record:  00001                              Flag: x
  Name:  Frank N. Stein,
 Title:                                     Date: 07-01-87
Company:  Spiderweb Productions            Mr/Ms: Mr.
Address-1:  1840 Shelley View,            Phone-1: 099-1234-759
Address-2:  Adaville,                     Phone-2:
Town/county:  GOTHICK, POTTS. PT72 5EN
Country:
Keyword-1:  Work        Note-1: Web spinner, brain surgeon
Keyword-2:  Hobbies     Note-2: Creative biology, computing
Keyword-3:  Car(s)      Note-3: Owns '67 Stashmobile


Record:  00003                              Flag:
  Name:  Poppy F. Lower, Dame
 Title:                                     Date: 07-01-87
Company:  Trendytops Ltd.                  Mr/Ms: Ms.
Address-1:  Shady Nook, Lower lane        Phone-1: 092-7162-544
Address-2:  Thistledo,                    Phone-2:
Town/county:  Narkville, RUTS. Z95 2QR
Country:
Keyword-1:  Work        Note-1: Creative neckwear
Keyword-2:  Hobbies     Note-2: Welding woodwork, car repairs
Keyword-3:  Car(s)      Note-3: '86 Fiat, '82 Alfa Romeo
```

■ SECTION 56
Sublists

8 When you return to the main record form, you will see ticks in the eight boxes at the right-hand side where you have pressed the + key. These indicate that this record forms part of the two sub-menus, Business and Computer-owner.

9 Similarly, record 2 is marked in box 2 (Personal), and record 3 is marked in boxes 2 and 3 (Personal and Computer-owner).

10 When you have marked in the sub-menu items, leave the list by pressing Esc if you want to print lists.

11 When you use the RECORDS TO PRINT menu, you will now see the sub-menu names in the list. You can select to print records that are in these categories — for example, Computer-owners. Remember to choose a suitable print format — proof record is often the best for this purpose. As always, it takes a long time for the program to select the records.

12 Unfortunately, when such a selective list is printed, the basis of selection (such as Computer-owner) is not shown.

SECTION 57
Manipulating records

Sublists allow a Master list to be manipulated in ways that, with some ingenuity and a lot of hard work, make them very useful. In particular, a lot of work on the screen can be done to select records for viewing, and you can pick records that conform to a particular specification, like all computer-owners in Watford.

All of this can be done on screen, and if you later want printed lists, you can specify that a set of records will be marked with a key letter. You might, for example, specify that all computer-owners in Watford be marked W.

You can then print out such lists by printing the records with a W key, or, of course, you can use the names and addresses for envelopes or labels, or list the telephone numbers.

All of this requires the use of yet another menu, and a new set of items to choose. For an example, we will stay with the PEOPLE file, but if you want to gather experience for yourself, you should start by making a much longer file of records, as complete as possible, that will be of use to you.

1 Select Mailing list from the opening menu, put in the disk, and take the BEGIN DATA ENTRY option. This assumes that you have selected the correct file (such as PEOPLE) to work with.

2 You will see the first record of your file. Press the F2 key to see a menu for data entry. Your options are:
Add record
Delete record
Begin search
End search
Customise data entry
Flag records
Update sublists

3 As a first example, select the BEGIN SEARCH option and press RETURN. You will see a blank report form. You can fill in any item — try Lo for LAST name.

4 Now press Ctrl-RETURN. The screen finds the corresponding entry, the surname 'Lower'. If there are any other entries in YOUR list, like Lovelace, Loughton, Loss, Lough, etc., you will see them in order of record number as you press the PgDn key. If you have sorted the records into any other order, you will see them in that order.

5 To stop the search, you must press the F2 key again and select END SEARCH. This will leave the last selected record on screen.

6 You can match any of the items in the main form in this way, and also specify sublist items. If you have ticked sublist items, then you will not get a list of all records in which these appear, but you will get a list in which each record consists of these groups. For example, you can't specify all records with Sublist 1 ticked, but you can get a list of all records in which the surname starts with Sm and Sublist 1 is ticked.

7 You can search for a match with more than one item. For example, you can type Ac for Last name, and Nutt for town, and get a match for every record that uses BOTH of these. For example, you will get Accurist in Nuttlebury, Actor in Nutterwick and Acerbic in Nuttleston, if these records exist in your file.

8 Be careful to check all the boxes in the Search form to make sure that you are not restricting your search too closely. It's particularly easy to neglect ticks in the sublist boxes.

■ SECTION 58
Marking records

The search action of the **Data entry menu** can also be used to mark records out for subsequent processing. As always, a small file can be used only for illustration, but if you have created a longer file, then this feature can be really useful.

1 With the records on view, press the F2 key to get the DATA ENTRY menu.

2 Move the shaded bar to FLAG RECORDS, press RETURN.

3 You will see a blank entry form, with the extra line:

Flag to be used at the top. Enter this letter, which should be one that reminds you of what the flag means (S for special importance, for example).

4 The rest of the form is used as before. You enter names or fractions of names that will select some records from the file.

5 Press Ctrl-RETURN to flag all the affected files with this letter. You can now use this flag letter to select items for lists of all kinds, whether printed or on screen.

The example shows a record flagged with the letter S in this way.

Note that there is no way of searching for or flagging any combinations other than the AND type. In other words, you can look for Smith AND Watford, but you can't look for Smith OR Watford.

```
                        PROOF REPORT

      Record: 00002                      Flag:  S
        Name: Donald R. Acula,
       Title: Chairperson                Date:   07-01-87
     Company: Androgenoids Ltd.         Mr/Ms: Mrs.
   Address-1: Hammer House, Anvil Lane  Phone-1: 087-2414-599
   Address-2:
Town/county: Nuttingham, Tutts. T87 2NQ
     Country: England
   Keyword-1: Work          Note-1: Robotics
   Keyword-2: Hobbies       Note-2: Theatre, sewing, weaving
   Keyword-3: Car(s)        Note-3: '86 Metro, '79 Porsche
```

➤

■ SECTION 59
Refinements

There are a number of useful refinements that we have skipped over so far in order to gain experience more rapidly. One of these is the extent-of-file indicator. This is the double-headed arrow at the top of the form which is used to show how far you are in a file of records. The distance through the file is measured by the distance of the arrow from the left-hand side.

For a short file, this can give a quite accurate representation of how far you have travelled through a file. Even for a large file, it is still useful.

The extent of file arrow is particularly useful when you have sorted a file other than by record number. It can show, for example, how far through the file you have had to search for an item, or how much of the file is left to look for more.

Another useful feature is the ability to speed up data entry by customising the form. As it stands, each press of RETURN or down-arrow will move the cursor to another field. This field might never be required (there's no point in using the Country field if all your customers are in Essex, for example), or a field such as Town might always be the same (all your customers are in Colchester).

To customise data entry:

1 Bring up the records that you want to work on, or create a new Master list.

2 Select Data entry, and then press the F2 key when ready. Select the CUSTOMISE DATA ENTRY line.

3 You will see a blank data entry form. You can at this point put in one of four letter codes in selected fields. These are:

    S to skip a field. This is very useful to avoid excessive key-pressing.

    C to copy a field, if all entries are in the same town, for example. Using C makes the cursor stop at this field in case you want to change it.

    D to duplicate a field; as for C, but the cursor does not stop.

    H to hide the field; the cursor does not stop, so the field can't be changed.

■ **SECTION 59**

Refinements

4 Mark the field as needed. The most useful marker is S because it allows you to skip the fields that will never be used. When you have finished marking, press Ctrl-RETURN to record the customising. NOTE that if you simply press RETURN, the menu will return in the usual way, but your customising work will not have been recorded and will have no effect.

The final item in the Data entry menu allows you to Update sublists. This does not allow you to edit the sublists – it allows you to remove selected records from sublists.

1 Select the UPDATE SUBLISTS option, press RETURN.

2 Enter in the blank record form anything you need to select a group of records, such as a name, a town, etc.

3 Move over to the sublists box with Ctrl-right arrow and put a hyphen in each box that you want this record removed from. In our example, putting a hyphen in Box 2 removes all matching records from the Personal sublist. You can also use the + key to add a sublist box to the selected records.

4 Move back to the main form with Ctrl-left arrow, and press Ctrl-RETURN to carry out the updating. This can take a considerable time on a long file.

■ SECTION 60
Deleting records

Deleting a record is a two-part process. This has been done deliberately so that you will think twice about deleting data that might still be of use to you. The first part of deleting removes a record from the list, but does not remove it from the disk, which is the second part.

1 Use the normal steps of selecting Data entry to display the record that you want to remove. Use key F2 to display the Data entry menu.

2 From this menu, select DELETE RECORD. Press RETURN.

3 This deletes the record as far as normal use of this Master list is concerned.

When several records have been deleted in this way, you should remove them from the disk as well. To do this you need to need to return to the MailList main menu.

1 Select MANAGE MASTER LISTS.

2 From this menu, select PURGE DELETED RECORDS. Press RETURN.

3 You will be asked to wait until deleted records are purged from the disk. This takes a considerable time, and there will be a lot of activity from the disk drive.

4 A message will tell you how many MLD records have been purged, and how many files are in use. You are then asked to press RETURN to end the process.

More dots

Dot commands can also be used in the word-processed files that are operated with MailList. This is not mentioned in the HELP pages, and some examples might be useful.

Here is a standard form letter which includes some dot commands that we have not illustrated before:

```
.cs
.av"Item",thing/o
 Dear &first/o&,

     Have you a copy of &thing/o& because I
seem to have lost mine.

                    Ian.
```

The **.cs** command means 'clear screen', so that a message can be typed on a clear screen — the command exists, but is not really needed for WordStar 1512.

The **.av** command means 'advise from keyboard'. This is a way of making the program stop and wait for something to be entered from the keyboard rather than from a prepared file.

The form of the .av command is very different from anything else so far, and is a throwback to other versions of WordStar. Like any other dot command, .av must be on a line of its own. It is followed by a variable name, but this is *not* chosen in the usual way from the list in the F2 menu. This same variable name is also put into the text where it will be used.

The variable name that is put following .av must consist of a name using normal alphabetical letters, but not one of the standard set. *The name must end with* /o (slash-oh).

In the text, the position for the word or phrase that will be entered from the keyboard is marked by using the variable name. In this case, the name is surrounded by two ampersands (&).

When the standard letter is printed, you are asked, before each letter is produced, for the phrase that will be allocated to (in this example) thing/o. When you type the name or phrase, the whole letter is produced.

■ SECTION 61
More dots

By putting a phrase in quotes as part of the .av command, this phrase will be made to appear on the screen as a reminder of what you need to type.

```
Dear Jim,

        Have you a copy of Guide to Crustacea
because I seem to have lost mine.

                    Ian.




Dear Fred,

        Have you a copy of Gulliver´s Travels
because I seem to have lost mine.

                    Ian.




Dear Sid,

        Have you a copy of Gas and gasbags
because I seem to have lost mine.

                    Ian.
```

Another dot command of MailList is **.DM** which can be followed by a message. For example .DM Printing list of defaulters. This allows the screen to remind you of what the printer is doing during a MailList operation.

PART EIGHT

Odds and ends

■ SECTION 62
Document mode

In the CHANGE SETTINGS menu of WordStar 1512, turning to WORD PROCESSING SETTINGS, you will find one choice called DOCUMENT MODE. The HELP key is not exactly helpful about this, and since you might very easily need to make use of it, some explanation might be useful.

Document mode is normally switched on. When this is the case, WordStar 1512 is set up for word processing normal documents such as letters, memos, book script and so on. This implies documents that are organised into standard-sized pages and formatted for printing in the normal way.

One of the advantages of using a word processor such as WordStar 1512, however, is that it can read material that has been prepared by other programs. We have dealt earlier with methods of reading and working with text files from other editors. In addition, WordStar 1512 can work with files that have been created by the well known spreadsheet programs such as SuperCalc, Lotus 1 − 2 − 3 and Symphony.

To read files in from these programs, you need to work in non- document mode. The reason is that you don't know in advance how wide a spreadsheet file may be, or how it is organised. The last thing you want is to have your word processor reorganise a spreadsheet display into pages that would never rearrange into the original format. To read such a file, proceed as follows:

1 From the opening menu select CHANGE SETTINGS and from this, select WORD PROCESSING SETTINGS.

2 Move the shaded bar to DOCUMENT MODE and press the Del key. This will cancel document mode. Press RETURN to fix this setting in memory.

3 From now on, all documents will be created in non-document mode. If you want to return to normal word processing settings, you will have to re-set document mode in the WORD PROCESSING SETTINGS menu by typing a + at the appropriate place.

4 Get back to the Opening menu, and select WORD PROCESSING. If you need a demonstration file, put the Text & Data disk into the drive you use for data. One file on this disk, called ROBINS.WKL, is a small Lotus spreadsheet.

5 Choose a new filename, such as SPREAD, and wait for the editing screen to appear. You will find that the advice at the top of the screen has changed. There is no ruler line, to start with, and you now have printed on the top line two quantities, labelled as FC and FL.

6 The number following FC is the total number of characters in the file, taken from the start of the file to the present cursor position. The number following FL is the number of lines from the start of the file to the current cursor position.

7 There is no right margin set, no word-wrapping, no right justification, no page breaks, no reforming, and with no ruler you cannot alter tabs or set margins. You can make selections on Tabs and Margins, but they are not obeyed.

8 If you now read in a Spreadsheet file, you will see it on screen in the form that it would take if you were running a spreadsheet. Use the F2 key to select INSERT A FILE, and insert ROBINS.WK1 into your text.

9 WordStar 1512 automatically recognises this as a Lotus worksheet, and brings up a menu to suit. If you have used a SuperCalc or Symphony worksheet, you will get a corresponding message.

10 For the Lotus sheet, you are asked if you want to ACCEPT the range address, REVISE the range address, or SPECIFY whole worksheet. For this example, the range address corresponds to the whole worksheet, so that the default option (Accept range address) is suitable, and pressing RETURN will load in the worksheet.

11 These options allow you to incorporate only parts of a spreadsheet into your text, or a predetermined range, or a range that you specify. In general, these options will be comprehensible and useful only if you are familiar with one of these spreadsheets.

■ SECTION 63

ASCII files

WordStar 1512 normally records and reads documents that are in **ASCII** code. The letters are the initials of **American Standard Code for Information Interchange**, and the code is one in which each letter of the alphabet, punctuation mark and digit (0 – 9) is allocated a number code between 32 and 127 inclusive.

Decimal	Character	Hexa-decimal	Decimal	Character	Hexa-decimal
0	NUL	00	32	space	20
1	SOH	01	33	!	21
2	STX	02	34	"	22
3	ETX	03	35	#	23
4	EOT	04	36	$	24
5	ENQ	05	37	%	25
6	ACK	06	38	&	26
7	BEL	07	39	'	27
8	BS	08	40	(	28
9	HT	09	41	)	29
10	LF	0A	42	*	2A
11	VT	0B	43	+	2B
12	FF	0C	44	,	2C
13	CR	0D	45	−	2D
14	SO	0E	46	.	2E
15	SI	0F	47	/	2F
16	DLE	10	48	0	30
17	DC1	11	49	1	31
18	DC2	12	50	2	32
19	DC3	13	51	3	33
20	DC4	14	52	4	34
21	NAK	15	53	5	35
22	SYN	16	54	6	36
23	ETB	17	55	7	37
24	CAN	18	56	8	38
25	EM	19	57	9	39
26	SUB	1A	58	:	3A
27	ESC	1B	59	;	3B
28	FS	1C	60	<	3C
29	GS	1D	61	=	3D
30	RS	1E	62	>	3E
31	US	1F	63	?	3F

■ SECTION 63
ASCII files

Decimal	Character	Hexa-decimal	Decimal	Character	Hexa-decimal
64	@	40	96	`	60
65	A	41	97	a	61
66	B	42	98	b	62
67	C	43	99	c	63
68	D	44	100	d	64
69	E	45	101	e	65
70	F	46	102	f	66
71	G	47	103	g	67
72	H	48	104	h	68
73	I	49	105	i	69
74	J	4A	106	j	6A
75	K	4B	107	k	6B
76	L	4C	108	l	6C
77	M	4D	109	m	6D
78	N	4E	110	n	6E
79	O	4F	111	o	6F
80	P	50	112	p	70
81	Q	51	113	q	71
82	R	52	114	r	72
83	S	53	115	s	73
84	T	54	116	t	74
85	U	55	117	u	75
86	V	56	118	v	76
87	W	57	119	w	77
88	X	58	120	x	78
89	Y	59	121	y	79
90	Z	5A	122	z	7A
91	[	5B	123	{	7B
92	\	5C	124			7C
93	]	5D	125	}	7D
94	^	5E	126	~	7E
95	_	5F	127	DEL	7F

Notes:
(i) Codes 1 to 26 represent the codes for CONTROL-A to CONTROL-Z.
(ii) Code 35 is generally used to represent both the # and £ symbols.

➤

■ SECTION 63
ASCII files

Any document that is described as being ASCII (or **text**) will be in this code, and can be read by WordStar 1512. Conversely, WordStar 1512 creates documents in this form, and these can be read by other word processors. Note, however, that other word processors in the WordStar family need to be set to non-document mode to read ASCII files, and some other types of word-processing program also need to be set to non-document mode. This is usually a shorter and simpler procedure than in WordStar 1512.

If you have tried to read a MailList MLD file into a WordStar 1512 text file, however, you will have seen mainly a collection of strange characters. This is because MailList data files use codes outside the normal ASCII range of 32 to 127, and these codes, in standard WordStar 1512 files, correspond to the extra characters that you normally obtain by pressing the Alt key while typing a three-digit number.

■ SECTION 63
ASCII files

You can, however, convert such a file into ASCII form so that it can be printed. The procedure is as follows:

1 Make sure that the data disk that contains your MailList data files contains only MailList file COPIES. The conversion will affect all files on the disk. It does no harm to text files on the disk, becaused only files with the MLD extension are affected, but it takes time. The MailList files that are created by conversion will no longer be useful for MailList use, because they have the ASC extension. Your original files are, however, still in place. BE VERY CAREFUL IF YOU KEEP SUCH FILES ON HARD DISK.

2 From the opening menu, select MailList. From the MailList main menu, select MANAGE MASTER LISTS. On this menu, select CONVERT TO ASCII FORMAT.

3 You will be asked to select a drive and directory. if you are using a twin drive machine, you might select B for the drive, and \ for the directory. The \ choice will be added automatically if you press RETURN after typing the B letter.

4 When you press RETURN, all the files on the specified drive and directory will be converted. This is a fast operation, and you have no time for second thoughts.

5 You can now return to the opening menu and so to word processing. The directory of files will show that for each .MLD file you now have a corresponding .ASC file. These .ASC files can be read into text. It is better to use non-document mode if you are uncertain of the size of the files. They will usually extend beyond the screen limits, so that you have to use the right cursor movement to see the end of each line.

6 If you want to print such files, use a dot-matrix printer set to the minimum size of type (such as 17-point), and a line length of at least 132 characters. This can often be a useful alternative to a Proof report from MailList.

■ SECTION 64
■ Amending the dictionary

In Section 46 we noted that the Spell-check dictionary could not be altered except by the addition of words to the Personal dictionary. You can make amendments to the words that you have added for yourself into the Personal dictionary, because these are held in a separate section that is not protected.

Nevertheless, it is not advisable to make changes even to this directory on the main Spell-check disk. The safest procedure is to copy the contents of the personal word list over from the main disk, alter them as needed, and then copy them back after you are sure that they are acceptable.

This also permits you to use a completely separate dictionary disk for your own words, and you can change settings so that this disk can be automatically selected for your personal dictionary rather than the file on the main disk in drive A.

First of all, we'll deal with copying the Personal word list from the Spell-check disk. This assumes that you have added some words, and want to change some or work with a separate disk of specialised terms.

1 Leave WordStar 1512 altogether, so that the prompt sign A: shows on screen. If in doubt, remove all disks, press Ctrl-Alt-Del, wait for the screen message and insert the MS-DOS disk when prompted. Remove this disk when the A: prompt shows.

2 Put a write-protect tab on to your DICTIONARY disk, No. 6. For a twin-drive machine, put this disk into drive A, and a formatted blank disk into drive B. For other machines, follow the normal procedure for copying a file from one disk to another. Hard disk users will be copying from hard disk to drive A.

3 Type this instruction (twin-drive machine):

COPY A:\1512\DICTIONARY\PERSONAL.DCT
B:PERSONAL.DCT

Check it very carefully, particularly for the space between the end of DCT and the following B:, then press RETURN.

4 This will make a copy of the personal dictionary on to the fresh disk. Label this disk as PERSONAL.DCT.

5 You can now use WordStar 1512 to read the file PERSONAL.DCT from this disk. It will consist of all the words that you have added to your dictionary in the course of spelling checks.

158

Amending the dictionary

6 You can now edit this word list as you please, changing the spelling of any incorrect words or adding words. Save the file under that same name of PERSONAL.DCT when you have completed editing.

7 You can now transfer the file back. Remove the write-protect tab from the DICTIONARY disk (description for twin-drive machines). Place this disk in drive A again, and the PERSONAL.DCT disk in drive B. Type the command:

COPY B:PERSONAL.DCT
A:\1512\DICTNARY\PERSONAL.DCT

– and press RETURN when ready. This transfers the file back to the DICTIONARY disk.

You may want to use the separate PERSONAL.DCT disk. If so, you will have to change some settings. Load in WordStar 1512, and select the CHANGE SETTINGS menu from the Opening menu.

1 Select DRIVE/DIRECTORY SETTINGS from this menu.

2 You will see the following:
Text files

B:\	PRACTICE

Personal dictionary

A:\1512\DICTNARY\	PERSONAL.DCT

Main dictionary

A:\1512\DICTNARY\	MAIN.DTY

Internal dictionary

A:\1512\DICTNARY\	INTERNAL.DTY

Mailing list file

B:\	SAMPLE.MLD

3 Move the shaded block with the down-arrow key until it is on the line that contains A:\1512\DICTNARY\ and type B for the drive letter (or whatever suits your system). Now move to the next position, and use the Del key to remove the drive path \1512\DICTNARY\, but leave the name PERSONAL.DCT.

➤

Amending the dictionary

4 You can change the name PERSONAL.DCT if you like to match the name of the file on your own personal directory disk if this is not PERSONAL.DCT.

5 Press RETURN to save the changes.

6 Now when you use spelling checking (twin-drive illustrated), put the text on the screen, put the main DICTIONARY disk in drive A, and your personal dictionary disk in drive B. If you use a hard disk, you will have specified that the personal dictionary wil be in drive A, because the main dictionary will be stored on the hard disk.

The spelling checker will now take its 'ordinary' words from the main dictionary on the DICTIONARY disk, but the extra words that you have added will be checked from your own disk. Note that this allows you to use a very large specialised dictionary that occupies a complete disk.

Note that you cannot store the main dictionary in the RAM-drive. WordStar sets up 200K of RAM-drive, but you need at least 271K for the main dictionary. Using this setting of RAM-drive does not leave enough memory for WordStar 1512 to operate in unless you have expanded the memory of your PC 1512 to 620K.

If you have expanded the memory, you can place the main dictionary in drive C (floppy disk machine) each time the program loads in. You must also specify that drive C will be used for this directory in the drive/directory setting menu. This makes much faster spell-checking possible. If you use a hard-disk, spell-checking will be fast in any case, so that the use of RAM-drive is not necessary.

■ SECTION 65
The Help pages

Most guides to WordStar 1512 or any other word processor show the commands in sets, often grouped by the type of action. It's more likely that when you are beginning, you would like some quick help in the form of an alphabetical list.

This is the arrangement that has been used for this set of HELP topics, and it makes it easier to display the range of options in a practical way. The dot commands of both WordStar and MailList have been included in the list, and the explanations are fairly brief — they are intended more as a reminder than as a complete guide.

If the explanation is not sufficient for you, you will have to seek further help either from this book or from the WordStar 1512 manual or the HELP pages. The entries that are marked ML are MailList dot commands. Note that dot commands can be placed anywhere in the text (to start headers and footers, for example), but must obey the normal dot rules of being allocated a line each on the screen (they are not printed), and starting at the first column.

If a different left margin is used, any relaying of text must not be allowed to shift the dot commands.

Abandon file   From text entry, press Esc, then select *Abandon changes*, press RETURN. This does not save file, and unless there is an older copy on the disk, you will be left with no file.

Accept range address   One of the three choices available when a file to be inserted is from a spreadsheet such as Lotus 1 – 2 – 3.

Add record(ML)   Add a record to a MailList master list. Obtained from F2 menu from *Begin data entry* choice in MailList.

Ask for variables(ML)   Use .AV in document. This MailList command forces the program to halt until you supply a suitable entry and then press RETURN.

Auto page number   Option in *Page layout* menu of *Change settings* menu. Also available from *Printing* menu and *List printing* menu.

Auto reform   Ensures that text obeys margin settings. Can be turned off by using *Word processing settings* menu from *Change settings* menu. Must be turned off if margins are to be changed in the course of a document. For entering spreadsheet files, use non-document mode.

Available choices   Selection of fonts, colours and special characters that a selected printer can use with WordStar 1512. Used in *Customise printers* menu from *Change settings* menu.

The Help pages

Back up a Master list(ML) Option from *Manage Master lists* menu of MailList. Allows a backup copy of a Master list to be made. This backup copy cannot be used directly — *see* Restore Master list.

Beep during data entry(ML) Default setting for MailList data entry, changed from *MailList settings* menu.

Begin at Allows page numbering to begin at any selected page, default 1. *See* Printing menu, Modify print options.

Begin printing current file First option in *Printing* or *List printing* menu. Permits printing to begin when RETURN is pressed. Make sure that the current file is the one you want.

Begin search(ML) Option in *MailList Data entry* menu (F2 key). Allows you to enter criteria for a search through Master list.

Block menu Obtained by pressing F2, first page. Allows Move text, Copy text, Delete text, Restore text.

Boldface Use F2, page 1. Practically all printers support this. Appears brighter on screen.

Bottom margin Default is 8 lines, changed from *Page layout* menu of *Change settings* menu.

Case-sensitive search(ML) Allows upper and lower case to be distinguished. For example, a search for 'previous' will not find 'Previous'. Selected in *MailList settings* menu from *Change settings* menu.

Centre text Type text, press F2, Page 2, select *Centre line*. Cursor can be placed anywhere in the line. Beware of shifting dot commands.

Change settings Menu from *Opening* menu, allowing settings for Word processing, Mail list, Drive/directory, Page layout, Printer setup and Customising printers.

Change text disk No special precautions, apart from waiting until drive is no longer active. To get directory of new disk, select *Choose/create a file* from word processing Main menu. Be careful about disk space — WordStar 1512 needs at least twice as much disk memory as the total number of bytes in the files.

Choose/create a file Option from *Word processing* menu that allows a file other than the current file to be selected for editing.

Choose file to print Option from *Printer* menu, allowing you to print any file from the data disk.

Choose printer   Allows you to select one of three printers to use with WordStar 1512. Selected from *Page Layout* menu of *Change settings* menu.

Choose a printer   Allows you to select, from a large list of printers, one to include in your shortlist of three. Use *Set up printers* menu from *Change settings* menu.

Choose record to print(ML)   Allows choice of all Master list, flagged items, or sublist selection. Selected from *List printing* menu.

Clear screen(ML)   Use .CS in text.

Clear tabs   Press F2, Page 2, select *Tabs & margins*. Place cursor over tab to be cleared and type C to Clear. You will see tab cleared from ruler line.

Comment   Place .IG or .. in text at first column and follow with comment that will not be printed. Comment is terminated when RETURN key is pressed. Use to keep notes on stock letters, etc.

Condensed print   Available on dot-matrix printers (NON PS 17). Use *Set up printers* menu. Right margin and tabs may have to be changed.

Conditional except(ML)   Advanced MailList action not dealt with here; allows MailList to skip an action or set of actions and go to the next section.

Conditional if(ML)   Advanced MailList action not dealt with here; allows MailList to test data and go to some action if test is satisfied.

Conditional page   Using .CP in text, followed by a number of lines ensures that the specified number of following lines will be kept together, and not split across a page. Useful for headings and tables.

Convert to ASCII format(ML)   Allows a Master list to be converted to ASCII so that it can be read by word processors. Use *Manage Master lists* from *MailList* menu.

Copy block   Press F2 key, Page 1, use *Copy text* choice.

Copy file   From opening menu, select *File management*. Select *Copy* option. You are prompted for name of file to be copied, and the new filename for the copy (which might be the same name but on another drive).

Copy text   Allows a block of text to be marked and copied to another part of the same file. Use *Edit* menu from F2 key.

■ SECTION 65
The Help pages

Current colours   Set of colours that can be printed by a colour printer if you have one. Obtained from *Set up printer* menu of *Change settings* menu. Must be preset from *Customise printer* menu.

Current fonts   Printer sizes/styles, such as 10-pitch, 12-pitch, 17-pitch, Italic, etc. Obtained from *Set up printer* menu of *Change settings* menu. Must be preset from *Customise printer* menu.

Current print extras   List of extra characters or effects that are obtainable from some printers. Obtained from *Set up printer* menu of *Change settings* menu. Must be preset from *Customise printer* menu.

Cursor movement   Use arrowed keys for single character/line movement. Use with Ctrl for word left or right. Use Home and End keys for top or bottom of screen, and PgUp, PgDn to scroll text past cursor. Use Ctrl-PgUp to get to start of text, Ctrl-PgDn to get to end.

Customise data entry(ML)   Allows the standard entry form for Master list to be modified so that items can be skipped, identical entries arranged, or entry barred. Use F2 key at Data entry of MailList.

Customise printer   Allows you to select features like fonts, colour printing and special characters, if your printer supports them. Select from *Change settings* menu.

Date format   Normally shown in US form (month-day-year), but you can enter a date in your own preferred style for MailList.

Delete   For characters, use Amstrad DEL keys, back or forward. Ctrl with DEL-left will delete a line.

Delete block   Use F2, Page 1, and select *Delete text*.

Delete file   From opening menu, select *File management*. From this menu, select *Delete*. You will be prompted for filename.

Delete record (ML)   Allows a record to be deleted from a Master list. Select from *Edit* menu (F2) of Data entry to MailList. Old deleted records should be purged to remove them from the disk.

Display message(ML)   Use .DM in text for MailList to display a message on the screen as a prompt for entry from the keyboard, or a reminder of what is about to be done.

Display sublist boxes(ML)   Default setting that allows the sublist boxes to appear on each record. Select by *Mailing List settings* from *Change settings* menu.

■ SECTION 65
The Help pages

Document file   A file that has been created by WordStar, or a compatible program, can also be used to read any ASCII files. Document file is the default – to change this, select *Change settings* from opening menu, then *Word processing settings*.

Double strike   Printer effect that can be used to provide boldface print.

Drive/directory   Option in *Change settings* menu that allows the default drive for text files, dictionaries and Mailing list files to be selected, along with default file names. Select from *Change settings* menu.

Edit current file   Default in *Word processing* menu. Other options are *Choose/create file* and *Help*.

End command(ML)   Advanced MailList action not dealt with here, uses .EF to mark the end of a set of test conditions.

End after   Allows printing to terminate after a specified number of pages. Using 9999 forces all text to be printed. Select from *Modify print options* menu of *Printing* menu.

End page   *Edit* menu (F2) option to put in end-of-page marker so that the printer is forced to take another page.

End search(ML)   Instructs MailList to stop search for records. Obtained from F2 menu of Data entry to MailList.

Entire Master list(ML)   Option in *List printing* menu, Choose records to print.

Envelopes(ML)   Format option for MailList printing. From *Pick print format* menu of *List print* menu.

Exit to system   Use *Quit* option at opening menu.

File directory   Shown when starting editing by selecting *Choose/create a file* option. Also available when a file is to be inserted. File directory is held in a small window, and you can use PgUp and PgDn to select different portions.

File insert   Use F2, page 2, *Insert a file*. You will be asked to position the cursor, then to choose a file to insert. A file can also be inserted during printing by using the .fi command.

File insert(ML)   Uses .FI followed by filename to show name of file to be used at this point in a MailList set of instructions.

Find word/phrase   Press F2, page 2, select *Find and replace*. You will be prompted for text of up to 30 characters, then answer *Replace?* question

■ SECTION 65
The Help pages

with −. The find action starts from the cursor position and goes to the end of the text. Each found text is flashed, and pressing RETURN finds the next occurrence. If you press Esc, the cursor is left at the last text found.

Find/replace   Press F2, page 2, select *Find and replace*. You will be prompted for text of up to 30 characters, then answer *Replace?* question with +. You are then prompted for Replace text, and then for automatic replacement. The find and replace action starts from the beginning of the text and goes to the end of the text.

Find/replace case sensitive   Option in *Word processing settings* of *Change setting* menu. Allows the find/replace action to distinguish between words that use upper case and words that use lower case. For example, a Find on 'case' would not find 'Case' if this option were in use. The default is off.

Find\replace whole word only   Option in *Word processing settings* of *Change setting* menu. Forces find/replace to work with whole words only.

Flag records(ML)   Option in F2 menu from Data entry of MailList. Allows records to be flagged for easy identification.

Flagged records(ML)   Option in *Choose records to print* menu of List printing. Allows record bearing selected flag letter to be printed.

Footer margin   All footers are printed on the bottom line of the page, unless specified by using .FM command.

Footer text   Use .FO followed by whatever words are to appear in footer. You can also use # for page number. Text is terminated by RETURN.

Header margin   All headers are printed on the top line unless .HM command has been used.

Header text   Use .HE followed by text that is to appear in each header from that point on. Text is terminated by RETURN.

Help menu   Press F1 for HELP at any point when a command has been selected. Use HELP index for browsing through HELP pages.

Insert   The insertion of a character at the cursor position is the default. To replace characters, press Ins key or use *Change word processor settings* menu to make this the new default.

Insert blank line   Press Ctrl RETURN.

Insert file   Use F2 menu of *Edit* in *Word processing* to specify a file to be inserted at the cursor position.

Insert file(ML)   Uses .Fl followed by filename to indicate that a file has to be inserted.

Interrupt   Use Esc key to get out of any action. This may not allow escape from some actions like printing or disk actions.

Italic print   Obtained on some dot-matrix printers, see *Set up printers* menu for details of what your printer can achieve with WordStar 1512.

Justification   Right-hand justification is switched on or off by using *Word processing settings* from *Change settings* menu.

Left margin   Set by using F2, Page 2, *Tabs and margins*. Unless you have a very pressing reason to do so, you should not change this margin. Note that this can affect dot commands. Normally, dot commands will be placed at the correct position when you enter them, but relaying the text will shift them to the new margin position. You should not change any margins while text is in place unless automatic reform has been turned off. Also set more permanently by using *Page settings* menu of *Change settings* menu.

Letters(ML)   Preset format in *Pick print format* menu of List printing.

Line spacing   Set with F2, Page 2, *Line spacing*. The line spacing (single, double or triple) is visible on screen as well as on the printer.

Locate last find/replace   Cursor is always left at the position of the text found or replaced when the Esc key is used to stop a find or replace action.

Lotus 1 – 2 – 3   Spreadsheet that can be read into WordStar 1512 edit page, using non-document mode.

Mailing labels(ML)   Print format for address list of MailList, from *Pick print format* menu.

MailList(ML)   Prepare text with ordinary word-processing editing actions. Prepare Master list of insertions by selecting *MailList* at Opening menu. Print lists by selecting *List printing* from Opening menu.

Manual reform   Text can be reformatted by using *Paragraph reform*, from F2 key menu. Cursor must be placed at the start of a paragraph when this is done, and each paragraph must be reformatted separately.

Margin at bottom   Set with *Page layout* menu from *Change settings* menu. Default is 8 lines. Can also use .MB followed by number. This will be the number of lines between the last text line and the bottom of the paper.

Margin at top   Set with *Page layout* menu from *Change settings* menu. Default is 3 lines. Can also use .MT to set number of lines between top text line and the position of the paper in the printer at the top of a page.

Modify print options   Menu from *Printing* menu.

Move block   Press F2 key, Page 1, *Move text*. Note that block must be correctly marked by pressing RETURN at each end of the block, and that the original block will be deleted after it has been moved.

Move file   Option in *File management* menu, allowing a file to be moved from one drive/directory to another.

Name/rename sublists(ML)   Allows sublist items to be named, or names changed. Select from *Manage Master lists* menu of MailList.

New page   Obtained by using *End page* option in F2 menu, or by putting .PA in text at a new line at the point where new page must be taken.

Non-document file   Used for reading spreadsheets, also for MailList files converted to ASCII. Selected from *Word processing settings* of *Change settings* menu.

Number of copies   Option in *Modify print options* menu from *Printing* menu.

Number pages   Default setting in *Page layout* menu of *Change settings* menu. Page numbers will appear, but not automatically. *See* Auto page number.

Omit page number   Use *Number page* option in *Modify print options* menu, *Printing* menu. Alternatively, place .OP command in text, following which the conventional page numbering will be omitted.

Page break display   Shows with a dotted line on screen where text will be broken across a page.

Page margin offset   Choice in *Modify print options* menu of Printing menu. This allows an extra margin to be provided when printing.

Page number   By default, pages are numbered starting at 1. Page number can be changed within text by using .PN followed by next number desired, or switched off using .PO. To put a page number into a footer text, use the hash (#). Also controlled by *Page layout* menu of *Change settings* menu, and *Modify print options* menu of *Printing* menu.

■ SECTION 65

The Help pages

Page offset Left margin set by offsetting printer head in each line. Obtained from *Page margin offset* option in *Modify print options* menu of *Printing* menu. Can also use .PO followed by number of columns. The default is 8 columns.

Paper length Set in terms of number of lines total (excluding lines used by printer to set top of print position) by *Page length setting* in *Page layout* menu of *Change settings* menu. Can also use the .PL command. The number here is the sum of text lines, top margin and bottom margin, but excludes the 6 line space between the top of a sheet and the printer head position. Default is 66 lines.

Paragraph reform Reformats text one paragraph at a time, as distinct from the automatic reformat, which works on the whole text. Obtained when needed from the F2 editing menu.

Pause for next new page Option in *Modify print options* menu to allow for single sheets to be used.

Port Name for connector from which printer lead is taken. For a parallel printer, this is LPT1, for a serial printer COM1. Change this only if you are using a serial printer.

Printer description Name given to printer other than manufacturer's name. An unusual feature of WordStar 1512 which is not likely to be used by many. Obtained from *Set up printers* menu of *Change settings* menu.

Print file Option from Opening menu to allow any file to be printed.

Print styles Allows different fonts, colours (if available) and the print effects (special characters) to be selected in text. Selected from F2 key while editing. Note that print effects are not visible on screen, but message bar shows where a print style has changed.

Proof report(ML) Choice in MailList to permit a printout of the Master list records. Obtained from *Pick print format* menu of List printing.

Prompts On-screen messages, such as 'Place cursor where you want to move text'. These can be suppressed by using the *Word processing* menu from the *Change settings* menu.

Purge deleted records(ML) Allows deleted records to be removed from a disk. Selected from *Manage Master list* menu of MailList.

Quit Leave WordStar 1512 and return to DOS. Opening menu choice.

Reform To reform or reformat one paragraph of text, use *Paragraph*

169

relay from F2 menu. Normally, reform is automatic. Watch out for reforming of dot commands if the left margin has been shifted.

Rename file   Obtained from *File management* menu of *Change settings* menu.

Restore a Master file(ML)   Allows a backup Master file to be restored for normal use. Obtained from *Manage Master lists* menu of MailList.

Restore deleted text   Allows text deleted by block command or line delete to be restored to cursor position. Only the most recently deleted text can be restored. Obtained from F2 menu.

Right margin   Set with *Tabs & margins* menu from F2 menu. Margins should not be changed while text is being edited unless auto-reform has been turned off.

Rotary cards(ML)   Option in *Pick print format* of List printing. Puts record data in form suitable for card index.

Ruler display   The line display above the text which shows margins, columns and tab settings.

Save and continue edit   Is useful when working on a long document, as it allows you to save at intervals in case of power failure. Use *Save* option in *Editing* menu, F2 key.

Save and new file   Used to save one document and return to choose another filename. Press Esc and select to save text.

Screen movement   Position of screen relative to text can be shifted up/down by using PgUp and PgDn keys.

Select Master list(ML)   Option from *Manage Master list* menu of MailList. Allows selection of Master list filename.

Set tabs   Tabs are set from *Margins & Tabs* menu, obtained from F2 key.

Show sublist names(ML)   Option from *Mailing List settings* of *Change settings* menu.

Spelling correction   Summons spelling correction program by using F2 key option.

Sublist(ML)   Option in *Choose records to print* menu of *List printing* menu. Allows records to be chosen by sublist topic.

Subscript   Select from F2 menu.

The Help pages

Superscript Select from F2 menu.

Tabs & margins Allows setting of tabs and margins in the ruler line. Margins should not be reset while text is in the memory unless auto-reform has been turned off.

Telephone directory(ML) Output option of List printing that prints names and telephone numbers. Select from *Pick print options* menu of List printing.

Temporary indent Indent that is effective on each line until RETURN is pressed. Obtained from F2 key during editing.

Top margin Number of lines between printhead position when paper is fed in, and first line of text. Paper position is normally with top edge one inch above printhead position. Set with *Page layout* menu of *Change settings* menu.

Underline Option from F2 editing menu.

Update sublists(ML) Allows sublists to be edited while entering data. Use F2 menu.

Use another printer Option offered at start of printing text. Choose from selection of three — if you have them!

Use form feeds Option in *Page layout* menu of *Change settings* menu for users of continuous stationery.

Variable names(ML) Names for words or phrases that will be inserted into a document from another file. Most are preset, some can be specified for use with the .AV command. Standard names are picked from the F2 menu.

Word-wrap Normal arrangement that avoids splitting words across lines.

■ APPENDIX 1
Self-starting

It is a distinct advantage if your WordStar 1512 program can start up by itself, because this will cut down the amount of work that has to be done when you start using the program.

When a disk is put into the computer in response to the request for a System disk, the computer will load in the Disk Operating System (DOS), and then try to find a file called AUTOEXEC.BAT on the same disk.

If such a file is found, then the computer reads it and obeys commands in this file as if they had been typed from the keyboard. This means that if you want to make the 1512 System disk self-starting, all you have to do is to add the command **WS1512** at the end of this file.

1 Start up WordStar 1512 in the usual way. When you are asked for a file to create, specify AUTO as the name.

2 With this filename for a new file, insert the file A:AUTOEXEC.BAT – you will need to put the 1512 System disk into the drive to read this file.

3 You will see that the default AUTOEXEC.BAT file consists of the lines:

KEYBUK
MOUSE

4 Add another line: WS1512, and press RETURN.

5 Now save this file.

6 Return to MS-DOS, and rename the file on the 1512 system disk that was called AUTOEXEC.BAT into AUTOEXEC.TXT.

7 Copy over the AUTO file to the 1512 system disk. Now rename this file as AUTOEXEC.BAT.

8 WordStar 1512 will now start automatically each time you use the 1512 system disk at switch-on or reset.

Note: the AUTOEXEC.BAT file can be created more directly, but this method ensures that you keep an exact copy of it on the 1512 System disk, under another filename, just in case you need it.

On my own AUTOEXEC.BAT file, I have deleted MOUSE, because I never use the mouse with WordStar 1512.

172

■ APPENDIX 2
Using MODE

When you use a slow printer with WordStar 1512 you may find that you get a message about being out of paper or off-line when you quite evidently are not. This is really a time-out message.

The computer tests at intervals to see if more characters can be sent to the printer, and if this is not possible within a reasonable time, a warning message is delivered.

The reason for the time out is that a printer buffer is in use, and this takes a long time to empty. The message does no harm, and you can resume printing with no problems, but it's appearance is irritating.

Fortunately, there is a remedy. By using the command:

    MODE LPT:,,P

you can prevent the time-out message from appearing.

This command can be added into an AUTOEXEC.BAT file, preceding WS1512, so that the command is activated before WordStar 1512 starts. This is definitely recommended if you have a slow printer with a buffer.

Index

Index

Index

Underlining, 43

Wordstar 1512:
  controls, simple, 23
  Help pages, 161
  installing, 18
  main menu, 22
  opening menu, 21
  self-starting, 172
Word-wrap, 49
Word-processing settings menu, 58
Working disks, 12, 14
Write-protection, 14